Stars and Flowers

THREE SIDED PATCHWORK

by Sara Nephew

Dedication

This book is dedicated to my husband, Dale. Together we build on what has gone before.

Acknowledgements

Special thanks to Marian Garton, who volunteered to type and make changes.

Special thanks to Mary Hickey, who enjoyed the technique so much she designed a pattern for this book. (See pg. 44)

Special thanks to Rose Herrera, who did some quilting "just for fun."

Credits

Photography by Carl Murray
Illustrations and graphics by Jean Streinz
All quilts made by the author unless otherwise noted

Stars and Flowers: Three Sided Patchwork©

© Sara Nephew 1989

Library of Congress Card Number 88–72380
ISBN: 0–9621172–0–X

Contents

Preface

This book results from my efforts to make a Feathered Star quilt from 60° triangles. In working on this project I discovered a wonderful array of other quilt designs, some of which looked more like floral applique than stars and snowflakes.

I have called the method presented in this book "three–sided patch-work" because many of the designs must be pieced, from the center out, in threes. Most of them begin with a triangle to which a piece is added on each side, forming a larger triangle to which pieces are added on three sides, etc. Addition of the final pieces turns these quilts into the more familiar rectangles. Some of the quilts are not pieced in exactly this way, but are designed with the "three–sided patchwork" method in mind.

The basic unit of all these designs is the 60° (equilateral) triangle, my favorite three–sided figure. These triangles are fun to play with. They offer so many possibilities, so many quilts that haven't yet been made.

I hope you will enjoy the patterns given in this book, make the methods your own, and perhaps design even more "three–sided" quilts not yet imagined.

Introduction

The aim of this book is to provide all the information needed to make three–sided quilts and to make working with 60° triangles easy. The first part of the book presents the cutting and piecing methods used, general rules and formulas that apply to all 60° triangle quilts, and charts and tables to save the quilter time calculating fabric needs and strip and unit sizes.

Design methods are outlined next, for those wishing to try their hand at designing their own three–sided quilts. A gallery of photographs shows the 14 quilts for which patterns are given in this book.

The following section features quilt diagrams and step–by–step instructions for block and quilt assembly, including information on making other quilts using these patterns, and the templates needed for corner pieces. An index concludes the book, enabling readers to quickly locate any technique or subject.

I recommend that you read the book completely before beginning work on a particular quilt, as some terms or methods may be unfamiliar. Then choose a favorite quilt and work step–by–step. Happy piecing!

Tools

Two key tools go a long way in saving time when making three–sided quilts. The **Clearview Triangle** makes rotary cutting and accurate piecing of 60° triangles, 60° diamonds, hexagons, etc., fast and easy. The Triangle comes in three sizes. The **Clearview Half-Diamond** is designed especially for rotary cutting speed–pieced 60° diamonds divided lengthwise into two different fabrics. It also speeds the cutting of other shapes. These tools are made from 1/8″ acrylic, for use with a rotary cutter. (See page 56 for ordering information).

Besides Clearview Triangles, required tools are: a rotary cutter, a cutting mat, and a clear, straight ruler like the Salem Rule or Omnigrid (for cutting strips). A large rotary cutter is preferred, since it saves muscle strain, cuts faster, and tends to stay on a straight line. I also like a ruler that measures 6″x12″ for my strip cutting method (see page 6). The shorter rule is less likely to move during cutting.

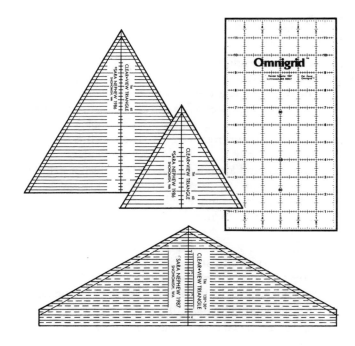

Rotary Cutting and Speed Piecing

For a little while, please set aside all thoughts of seam allowances, cardboard templates, and fabric as yardage. Consider only:

1. A strip of fabric;
2. A plastic 60° triangle with a ruled line on the perpendicular.

Every technique in this book is based on these 2 elements. The triangle is laid over the strip in various ways, and a rotary cutter is used along the edges of the triangle to cut off portions of the fabric strip.

Nothing in this book is difficult to do as long as the triangles and the strip are kept in mind. The strip may be changed by making it wider or narrower, or by sewing it to another strip before doing any cutting. The triangle may be changed by making it larger or smaller, or by changing it from a 60° (equilateral) triangle to a 120° half-diamond.

By working just with these elements, **many** shapes can be cut in whatever size desired. These shapes will all fit together to form a design, a quilt top.

After doing a large number of these quilts, I have found that it is not necessary to calculate all measurements each time a new design is cut and pieced. Instead, knowledge of a few basic rules often makes the next step automatic.

The following section first lists the rules and then describes the methods for cutting various shapes, emphasizing the rule for each operation. Please read through the whole section before beginning to piece any of the patterns in this book. The index at the back of the book offers easy access so you can review cutting methods while piecing a particular pattern.

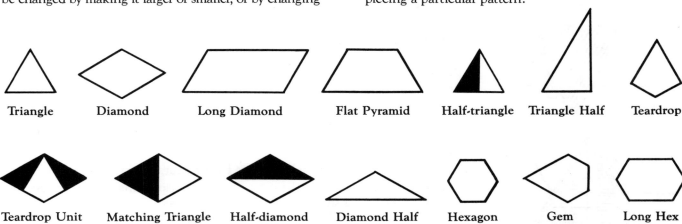

| Triangle | Diamond | Long Diamond | Flat Pyramid | Half-triangle | Triangle Half | Teardrop |

| Teardrop Unit | Matching Triangle | Half-diamond | Diamond Half | Hexagon | Gem | Long Hex |

*Rules

1. Before beginning to cut and piece a design, a **triangle size** is chosen to determine the scale of the design. The triangle size is the perpendicular measurement. A 3″ triangle measures 3″ from tip to base. (A **triangle size** is given for each pattern in the book.)
2. A triangle is cut from a strip whose width is the same as the height of the triangle's perpendicular.
3. Diamonds and long diamonds are cut from a strip ¼″ narrower than the strip a triangle is cut from.
4. Half–triangles, triangle halves and teardrops are cut from a strip ½″ wider than the strip a triangle is cut from.
5. To draft a hexagon, use a triangle measuring ½″ less than the **triangle size** chosen.
6. A hexagon is cut from a strip whose width is twice the perpendicular of the triangle used to draft the hexagon. (See hexagon table page 8)

All of the rules and measurements in this book apply if a ¼″ seam is taken.

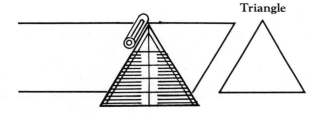

Triangle

Diamond

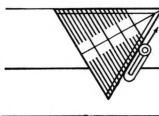

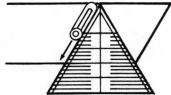

Cutting Strips

The first step in cutting any shape is cutting strips. All fabric should be prewashed. 100% cotton is preferred.

1. Fold fabric selvage to selvage and press. If pressing from the selvage to the fold produces wrinkles, move the top layer of fabric left or right keeping selvages parallel, until wrinkles disappear.
2. Bring fold to selvage (folding again) and press.
3. Use the wide ruler as a right angle guide, or line up the selvages with the edge of the mat, and the ruler with the mat edge perpendicular to the selvage. Cut off the ragged or irregular edges of the fabric.
4. Cut the strip width required, using the newly cut fabric edge as a guide.
5. Open the strip. It should be straight, not zig zag, if you had the ruler at right angles to the selvages and folds. Adjust the ruler slightly if necessary and trim fabric edges slightly before cutting the next strip.

To cut triangles:

Rule: A triangle is cut from a strip whose width is the same as the height of the triangles' perpendicular.
Example: A 3″ triangle is cut from a strip 3″ wide.

1. Position the tip of the Clearview Triangle at one edge of the strip, and the 3″ ruled line at the other edge of the strip.
2. Rotary cut along the 2 sides of the triangle. Move the Clearview Triangle along the same edge (do not flip it to the other side of the fabric strip) for the next cut, lining up the cut point of the fabric strip with the 3″ line on the plastic triangle. Check to be sure the strip edge is right along the ruled line.
3. Cut along both sides of the triangle. (Strips may be stacked up to 8 thicknesses and all cut at once.)

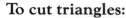

To cut diamonds:

Rule: Diamonds and long diamonds are cut from a strip ¼″ narrower than the strip a triangle is cut from.

1. Position the Clearview Triangle with one side along one edge of the strip. Strip should be ¼″ narrower than the triangle size chosen for the design. Cut the end of the strip to a 60° angle.
2. Reposition the Clearview Triangle so the tip is at one edge of the strip and a ruled line is along the other edge. (The same position as is used to cut triangles, except the strip is ¼″ narrower.)
3. Rotary cut **only** along the side opposite the first cut.
4. Keep moving the tool along the same side of the strip, lining up the cut edge and the side of the tool as shown. Always cut the side opposite the first cut. (Strips may be stacked up to 8 thicknesses and all cut at once.)

To cut long diamonds (and flat pyramids):

Rule: Diamonds and long diamonds are cut from a strip ¼" narrower than the strip a triangle is cut from.

Method #1
Trim one end of the strip to a 60° angle. Sew flat side of strip to the piece desired. Trim the other end to the correct angle.

Method #2
Trim one end of the strip to a 60° angle. Then measure one side of the strip according to directions, or to match the piece desired. Trim the other end to the correct angle.

Method #3
Position the Clearview Triangle over the fabric strip, lining up one edge of the strip with the measurement on the ruler as given in the pattern, or according to the instructions on page 12 for calculating the sizes of various shapes. Cut each side of the strip to obtain a flat pyramid, or cut one side, and mark the other side with pencil. Then trim it to a 60° angle to make a long diamond.

To cut a triangle half:

Rule: Half–triangles, triangle halves, and teardrops are cut from a strip ½" wider than the strip a triangle is cut from.

1. Cut triangles from a strip ½" wider than the **triangle size** chosen for the design.
2. Bisect these triangles on the perpendicular. Line up the side of the fabric triangle with the perpendicular line of the Clearview Triangle, then rotary cut the fabric triangle in half along the ruler edge.

To cut diamond half:

Use the Clearview Half–Diamond to rotary cut 120° triangles from the proper width strip. (See the table of measurements for half diamonds on page 10.)

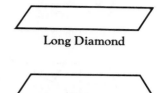

Long Diamond

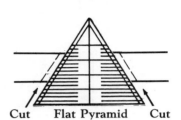

Flat Pyramid

Cut   Flat Pyramid   Cut

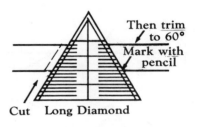

Then trim to 60°
Mark with pencil

Cut   Long Diamond

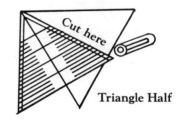

Triangle Half

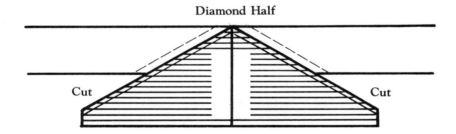

Diamond Half

Cut   Cut

Finding the Strip Width for a Half-Diamond or diamond half

(or see table page 10)

Use a fine-tipped pen or sharp pencil and slant it toward the ruler.

1. *Using the plastic template, draw your triangle.*
2. *Mark and draw the perpendicular line, extending it below your triangle's perpendicular.*
3. *Reverse the plastic template. Line it up along the extended perpendicular line, with the base line of the drawn triangle exactly under the same line less ½" on the plastic template (3½" for a 4" triangle.)*
4. *Draw one side.*
5. *Add ¼" seam allowance to the perpendicular line, extending sides to meet.*

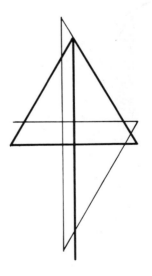

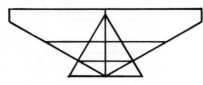

Cut Teardrop METHOD 1.

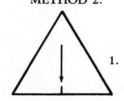

Cut Teardrop METHOD 2.

1.

2.

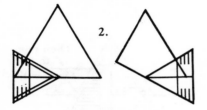

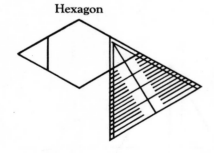

Teardrop Unit

Hexagon

To cut a teardrop:

Rule: Half–triangles, triangle halves, and teardrops are cut from strips ½″ wider than the strip a triangle is cut from.

Method #1

1. Cut triangles from a strip ½″ wider than the **triangle size** required.
2. Position Clearview Half–Diamond on triangle so its tip is opposite triangle tip. Line up the triangle point with the perpendicular of the Half–Diamond and line the triangle sides up evenly with one of the rulings, as shown. Then use rotary cutter to cut the base of the teardrop.

Method #2

1. Cut triangles as #1 above.
2. Measure the base of these triangles and find the center or half measurement.
3. Lay the perpendicular of the Clearview Triangle along the base of the fabric triangle, with the point at center. Rotary cut this wedge off. Reverse the template and cut off the other base corner.

Teardrop Unit

A teardrop unit, made from 1 teardrop shape and 2 triangle halves, is very useful. Seam one triangle half on each side of the teardrop to make a diamond-shaped unit. I line these pieces up for seaming at the bottom, not the top. Press each seam. Trim off the little seam ears to finish. This piece requires careful attention, both in cutting and seaming. If too small, narrower seam width is the solution.

Trim these off →

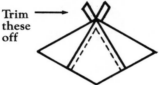

To cut a hexagon:

(It is usually not necessary to actually draft the hexagon.)

Two rules apply

Rule: To draft a hexagon, use a triangle measuring ½″ less than the **triangle size** chosen.

Rule: A hexagon is cut from a strip whose width is twice the perpendicular of the triangle used to draft the hexagon.

SEE TABLE BELOW

Example: 3″ **triangle size**—draft the hexagon from 2½″ triangles.

2½″ + 2½″ = 5″ strip. This will yield a hexagon that a 3″ triangle will sew on to.

1. Cut a fabric strip according to the pattern directions, or according to the hexagon table below.
2. Cut 60° diamonds from the strip. (See ''to cut diamonds'', pg. 6)
3. From each end of the diamonds, cut a triangle whose size is ½ of the strip width.

Example: 5″ strip means a 2½″ triangle must be removed from each end of each diamond.

HEXAGON TABLE

Triangle size	Drafting triangle	Strip to cut	Cut off triangle
1″	½″	1″	½″
2″	1½″	3″	1½″
3″	2½″	5″	2½″
4″	3½″	7″	3½″
5″	4½″	9″	4½″
6″	5½″	11″	5½″

Drafting Hexagons With the Clearview Triangle

To draft an accurate hexagon using the Clearview Triangle, two methods can be used. For method one:

1. Draw two sides of the triangle, marking the desired base line.

2. Extend these lines with a ruler.

3. Position the template along one line and draw the third intersecting line. Extend this line also.

4. Use a compass to draw a circle the marked distance along the lines. (Set the point in the center of the intersecting lines.)

5. Connect the lines at the compass markings.

Method two eliminates the compass. Simply mark the triangle base along each line and connect the marks. Either way, these hexagons include seam allowance.

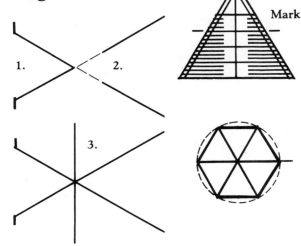

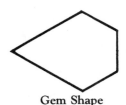

To cut a gem shape

Instead of cutting a hexagon from the diamond, cut only one point off, leaving this shape.

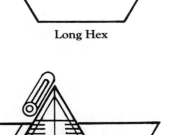

Gem Shape

To cut a long hex

1. Cut a strip width according to the HEXAGON TABLE.

2. Cut a long diamond (see pg. 7). The length of the long side is:

Triangle Size	Side Length
2″	4¼″
3″	7¼″
4″	10¼″
5″	13¼″
6″	16¼″

Long Hex

Cut one side, make a pencil mark at the other side, and cut to a 60° angle at this pencil mark.

3. From each end of the long diamond, cut a triangle whose size is ½ of the strip width. (Same as **cutting a hexagon**, page 8.)

(The long hex is not used in any of the patterns given in this book, but could be used in many designs. Example shown.)

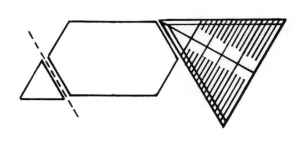

Cut Long Diamond

Mark

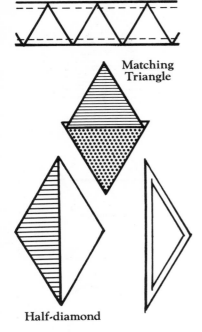

Matching Triangle

Half-diamond

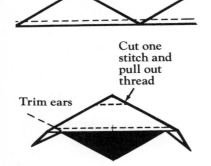

Cut one stitch and pull out thread

Trim ears

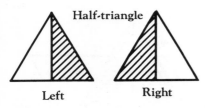

Half-triangle

Left | Right

Measure from center to edge at new triangle measurement after applying rule #4

ex. 3″ triangle becomes 3-1/2″

Seam Lines | Pencil Line

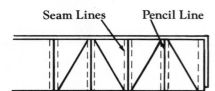

Sandwich Piecing

To sandwich piece matching triangle units (sandwich piecing uses 2 strips of fabric):

1. Cut strips of fabric the width of the triangle size. Two different fabrics are used, usually one light and one dark. Seam these strips right sides together with a ¼″ seam down both the right and the left side of the pair of strips. Position the Clearview Triangle so the tip is at one edge of the strips, and the ruled line for the correct size triangle at the other edge. Rotary cut on both sides of the tool. (Same as cutting triangles.)

2. Pull the tips of the seamed triangles apart and press open.

To sandwich piece half–diamond units

1. Cut strips of fabric whose width equals the perpendicular measurement of one-half the unit desired, including seam allowance, or according to the measurements given in the half–diamond table below. Two different fabrics are used, usually one light and one dark.

2. Sew light and dark strips right sides together with a ¼″ seam allowance down each side.

3. Using a Clearview Half–Diamond and a rotary cutter, cut triangles from the seamed strips. Line up the ruler tip at one seamed edge, and the desired line on the ruler at the other edge, and cut as for triangles.

4. Use a seam ripper to cut one stitch at the seamed tip of the fabric 120° triangles.

5. Pull the tips of the seamed triangles apart and press open, pressing across the width of the diamond and pulling the top and bottom out straight while pressing.

6. Trim off the little seam ears as shown.

HALF-DIAMOND TABLE

Triangle Size	Strip Width	Triangle Size	Strip Width
2″	$1^1/_4$″	5″	3″
3″	$1^7/_8$″	6″	$3^1/_2$
4″	$2^3/_8$″		

To sandwich piece half-triangle units:

Rule: Half-triangles, triangle halves, and teardrops are cut from a strip ½″ wider than the strip a triangle is cut from.

1. Cut two fabric strips ½″ wider than the **triangle size.** Usually a dark and a light are used. Press these right sides together.

2. On the Clearview Triangle, measure ½ the base of the triangle with the perpendicular measurement of the two fabric strips, OR USE HALF-TRIANGLE TABLE BELOW.

3. On the light colored fabric, draw lines as far apart as ½ the base of this triangle. Pencil, chalk or washout blue lines are all fine.

4. Seam through both strips ¼″ away on both sides of all the lines drawn. Press flat again.

5. Cut triangles from the strips, lining up the perpendicular of the ruler with the drawn line, and cutting as for triangles.

6. Bisect each triangle on the drawn line, using a rotary cutter or scissors. Pull tips apart and press open. This yields right and left half-triangle units.

HALF-TRIANGLE TABLE

Triangle Size	Strip Width	Distance Between Lines
2″	$2^1/_2$″	$1^1/_2$″
3″	$3^1/_2$″	$2^1/_8$″
4″	$4^1/_2$″	$2^5/_8$″
5″	$5^1/_2$″	$3^1/_4$″
6″	$6^1/_2$″	$3^{13}/_{16}$″

Fill-in Pieces for Stars

Fold yardage along selvages and press. Trim end straight across. Use cutting board and ruler as guides. Using a Clearview Triangle to get the correct angle and another ruler to make sure the angle side is long enough (the length of the side of your star point plus an inch or two), mark the line with pencil and cut.

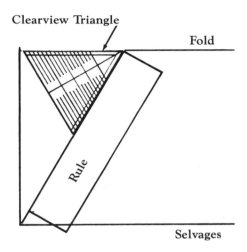

Note: To make economical use of fabric, cut background fill-in pieces first when possible. If this is not possible, add ¼-½ yd. to the background color.

Measure the next edge by folding the angled edge still attached to the yardage up to the top fold. Notch the fold where the point ends, and cut straight across the yardage there, cutting pieces apart at fold. This will provide three of the six fill-in pieces required around the star. For other pieces, repeat the above procedure in reverse or use the pieces already cut as patterns.

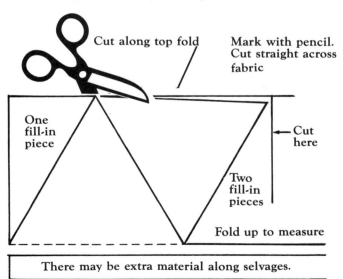

Straightening Star Edges

To straighten star edges, fold the star medallion across the middle, matching star tips, etc. Pin as necessary to keep the parts of the star lined up with each other. Mark and trim top and bottom edges parallel with the fold. You can use a mat, cutting guide, and rotary cutter. Leave as much fabric on the medallion background as possible.

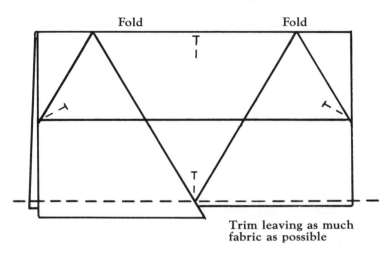

Without unfolding, leaving most of the pins in place, fold the other two sides together. Mark and trim the remaining raw edges parallel with the second fold and at right angles to the other trimmed edges. Use a Quilters Window, Salem Rule, or T-square. Leave as much fabric on the medallion as possible. More can be trimmed later, if necessary.

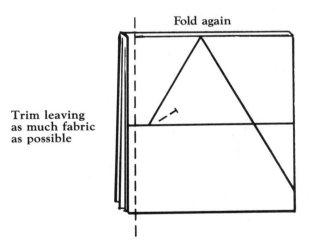

To find the size for cutting star background shapes for an original design or one in which the **triangle size** has been changed, begin to piece the star from the center out. When a star point has been pieced, measure one side of it and add 2″ or 3″ (float space around the star). This is the proper length to cut the fill-in pieces.

Enlarging or Shrinking a Pattern

It's fun to try substituting a different **triangle size** when piecing a particular quilt design. Following are instructions on how to do a rough estimate of how altering triangle size will change the size of the quilt. (To calculate new dimensions exactly, see pg. 15).

The new perpendicular triangle measurement is easy to figure. Just subtract ¾" from the triangle size chosen to obtain "finished'" height and multiply by the number of triangles perpendicular across the grid of the quilt design. (If this is not easily seen, sketch the design on graph paper.)

By comparing the new measurement with the original, you can then estimate the other dimension of the quilt. Let's use TRIANGLE STAR (pg. 16) as an example.

The body of the quilt, without borders, has 12 perpendicular triangles across the width. Using a 3" **triangle size,** the quilt width is 27" (2¼"×12) without borders. Changing to a 2" triangle size results in a width of 15" (1¼"×12) without borders, almost ½ the width of the larger quilt. Half the width and ½ the length would mean a quilt about ¼ the size. In this quilt, the change would be from a baby quilt to a doll quilt by reducing one triangle size.

To substitute a new triangle size follow the RULES and CUTTING DIRECTIONS for all the standard pieces. For larger pieces, or for flat pyramids, etc. the following information and table will be helpful. Use this information to change the size of shapes or to find the size of a shape in an original design.

When a shape is on graph paper, it can be analyzed and its size determined using simple math. Count the **rows** in the shape.

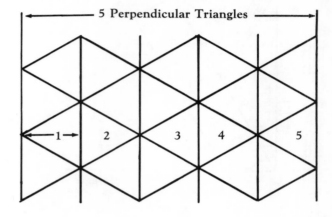

Example: This shape is composed of a triangle and a flat pyramid. Triangle cut from 3" strip, loses ¼" seam when sewed to flat pyramid. Flat pyramid cut from 2¾" strip, loses ¼" seam when sewed to triangle.

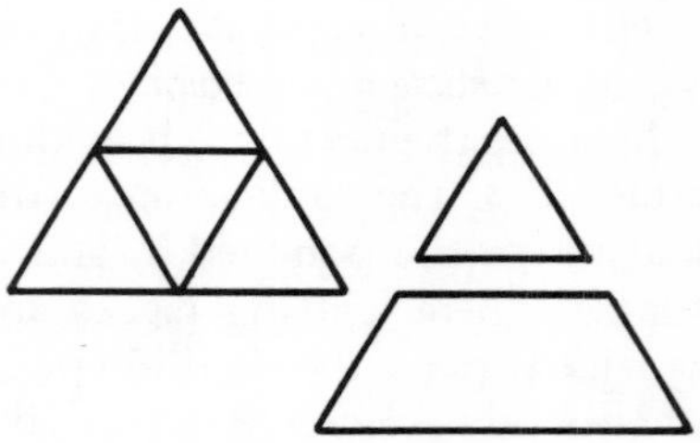

Result: 2¾" triangle height + 2½" flat pyramid height so shape is cut at 5¼" line on Clearview Triangle. (All the math in this example is based on a 3" triangle size).

COMMON SHAPES

Triangle size	Use this base line on the Clearview Triangle				
2"	3¼"	4¼"	5¾"	3¼"	4½"
3"	5¼"	7½"	9¾"	5¼"	7½"
4"	7¼"	10½"	13¾"	7¼"	10½"
5"	9¼"	13½"	17¾"	9¼"	13½"
6"	11¼"	16½"	21¾"	11¼"	16½"

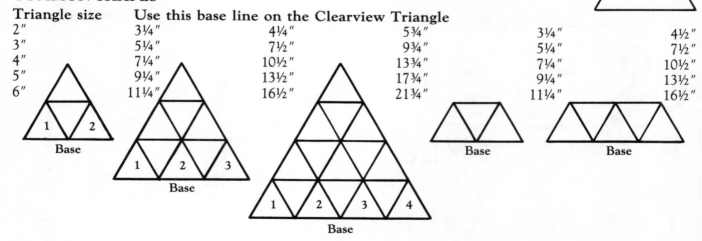

Example: To change a 2" triangle pattern to a 3" pattern, follow the tables above and when the dimension called for is 3¼", substitute 5¼".

Designing Three-sided Quilts

Three-sided quilts are concentric designs (based on a center point). Keep the basic units in mind (triangles, diamonds, teardrops, etc.), and begin on graph paper:

1. Start in the center with 6 triangles and work out, building a design. In each concentric row, decisions are made about repeat units, blank spaces, corners, etc. Each decision changes the design, so **many** different designs are possible.

2. Or start by drawing a star outline and then filling it in.

3. Or draw any shape that fits in the grid—a hexagon, star, diamond, or something different if you wish—and work both to the inside and the outside.

TURNING A DESIGN INTO A QUILT

Analyze the design to plan a piecing method. It is usually possible to plan for all straight-line sewing. Occasionally a piece will need to be set in and sewing will be from seam allowance to seam allowance. Sometimes the piecing will seem to be more work than the design deserves, and another design will be chosen. You can make a record of the piecing plan in two simple ways:

1. Lines can be drawn on the design indicating the various sections to be pieced.

2. Or, the design can be cut apart (I make a copy of my sketch and cut it apart, leaving the original intact) and glued to a background paper as kind of an exploded version, showing the sections and indicating the order in which they would be pieced and seamed together. Numbers can indicate assembly order if necessary (see Quilt Diagrams).

Before buying fabric and piecing the quilt, it is necessary to choose the scale in which the design will be worked out, from miniature to king size. Some patterns look better in a larger scale, or maybe you have a bed to cover. Some designs look better on a smaller scale, or maybe you want to experiment and learn without committing a lot of material to the project.

The triangle size you choose will determine the size of the finished project. You can use the rules given in this book to calculate the fabric required, as well as all the pieces that you will need to cut.

CALCULATING FABRIC REQUIREMENTS FOR AN ORIGINAL DESIGN

Once triangle size is decided, the rules and tables given in this book make it easy to determine how many yards of each fabric are needed. Every shape is cut from a certain width strip. Estimate how many of each shape can be cut from each strip, then divide that number into the total number of each shape needed. You will then know how many strips in this width you will need. Multiply the number of strips by the width in inches, divide by 36″ to determine number of yards, and round to the next larger quarter or half yard to allow for shrinkage. Add a bit more if you really like the color.

DESIGNING BORDERS

This grid only shows the vertical rows of the graph paper, brought around to all four sides of a design. The same could be done with the diagonal rows or the horizontal direction of the graph paper.

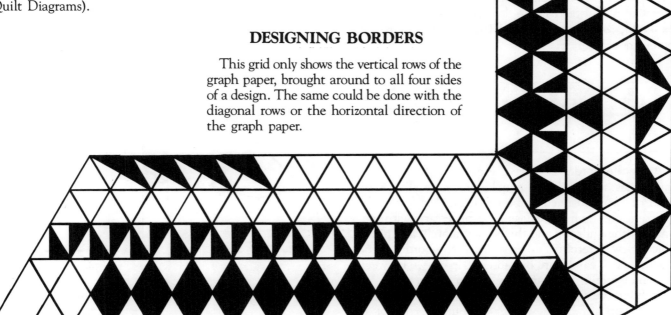

Designing Borders for Three-sided Patchwork

The right border can transform a merely pretty quilt into an outstanding one, finishing it with a perfect frame. The choices involved in deciding on a border are many. The shapes of the border should relate to the shapes in the center design. The heaviness or lightness of the border should complement the strength or airiness of the center. The border design can be drawn on graph paper and laid along the edge of the graphed quilt, or can be held up in the air at a distance from the pieced quilt to get a feel for how well they go together.

After the artistic decisions have been made, some thought must be given to fitting the borders on to the center of the quilt. One often workable solution is to make the background fabric of the center larger than it needs to be so that it can be cut down to fit the pieced borders. Care must be taken, however, not to:

1. Make the finished quilt too large; or

2. Leave visually unattractive excess space around the center design. This method definitely will work if you plan ahead enough to do it. A similar approach is to add strips of fabric to the center to bring it up to the border size.

Theoretically, the quilter can change the size of the triangle used to piece the border, in order to achieve a mathematically perfect fit. However, having the border look larger on two sides and smaller on two sides does not appeal to me. You may want to try it.

Some other changes in the border can work as excellent fitting tools. **Vertical strips** incorporated into the border design often help adjust the borders to fit the quilt. A **center piece** in the border design can be varied and adjusted to help the border fit the quilt. For example, the center piece of the peppermint ROSE border could be:

After the border is pieced, especially if it includes much bias in the edge, it may have stretched an extra inch or two and need to be eased on. Mark centers, quarters, etc. (as many divisions as necessary) with pins on both the quilt top and the border, match, and pin in place. Sew, stretching to ease on. If the border is too small, do not ease it on, but add a strip or two between design elements or enlarge the center piece.

Stabilize the eased-on border or ruffled bias edges with a final strip of fabric sewed to the outside edge of all borders. This strip must be cut on straight of grain. The length of this strip must equal the quilt measurement across the center either horizontally (the two short sides) or vertically (the two long sides). Mark these measurements, as well as centers, quarters, etc., pin in place, and ease the fullness of the border onto the final strip. Leave extra strip outside the marks for overlap or mitred corners.

Finally, press flat, using a hot iron and a wet press cloth. Especially if you have used 100% cotton fabric, the bias of the triangle pieces will help the border shrink back and flatten.

The most challenging part of designing borders for three-sided quilts is the corner. The shape required for the corner depends on the design used in the borders. Experiment to find the most attractive corner.

If you are using a border of matching triangles (SILHOUETTE), this is the shape required to fill in each corner. It can be accurately drafted using the following method: (see below).

1. Sew borders of matching triangles to the quilt top. Ends of borders will leave an opening. The 2 corner triangles must be the same color.

2. Lay a 90° corner ruler (Quilter's Window, Salem Rule, Omnigrid, etc.) over the opening, lining it up with the edges, to measure the distance from the corner to the triangles. Allow for seams.

3. Draw on paper or cut a fabric square to this measurement (4½″ square for 3″ triangle border). Then, using a Clearview Triangle, draw or cut away a 30° angle from the corner to the center on 2 adjacent sides of the square. This is the corner piece. This may be added to by inserting a triangle, teardrop, etc. Either applique it over the corner or draft the corner including the additional shape and make templates.

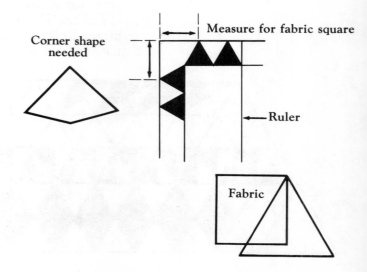

The Quilts

HOW TO USE THESE DIAGRAMS

The following illustrations look different from the finished quilts (shown in color on pg. 25-32) because they show a cut-a-part of the major sections of each design and how it is constructed. Each section must be pieced first, and then added on.

Cutting sizes are given in the pattern for the larger triangles, long diamonds, flat pyramids, hexagons, etc. Otherwise the **triangle size** used for the whole design, indicated at the beginning of the instructions for each quilt, is the basic measurement for all cutting and piecing techniques. Follow the rules and directions as indicated.

Begin by piecing and pressing the center unit, followed by the next three outside units, then the next three, etc. *(Note: If a star is being pieced, it is often more economical to cut the background fill-in pieces for the star first, getting the smaller pieces out of the remainder. If this is not possible, add ¼ to ½ yard to the background fabric.)*

Fabric requirements given for each pattern are for 45″ wide pre-washed cotton or cotton blends.

To make different quilts from these patterns, analyze the block or star in a particular quilt layout to see how many concentric rows it fills on equilateral graph paper. (See designing three sided quilts page 13). Any other block with the same number of rows can be substituted into the same quilt layout.

Determining Size of a Finished Quilt

To calculate the size of a finished quilt, two triangle measurements are needed: the perpendicular of the triangle without seam allowance (always ¾″ less than **triangle size**), and the length of the triangle **side** without seam allowances, which can be measured with a ruler on the Clearview Triangle. (Or use the table below.)

Multiply the "finished" perpendicular height by the number of triangles in one perpendicular line across the quilt. Multiply the "finished" triangle side by the number of sides across the other quilt dimension.

These two calculations will give you the measurements of the finished size of the quilt.

TABLE OF FINISHED TRIANGLES (when using ¼″ seams)

Triangle Size	Finished Perpendicular	Finished Side Length
1″	¼″	5/16″
2″	1¼″	1 7/16″
3″	2¼″	2 5/8″
4″	3¼″	3 13/16″
5″	4¼″	4 15/16″
6″	5¼″	6 1/8″
7″	6¼″	7¼″
8″	7¼″	8 7/16″
9″	8¼″	9 9/16″
10″	9¼″	10¾″
11″	10¼″	11 7/8″
12″	11¼″	13 1/16″

Note: The diagrams usually consist of combinations of the symbols for individual units (ex. half-diamond  *) showing proper placement in sections, rows, etc., rather than a sketch of how the seaming actually looks when incomplete. So 2 half-diamonds sewn together would be shown as number 1 rather than number 2 (which is closer to the way they might actually look). Also when individual instructions are not given for a triangle's size, it is the same as the triangle size given at the beginning of the pattern.*

Number 1

Number 2

Triangle Star

36″ x 42″ (3″ triangle size)

Fabric requirements:

1 yd. red
½ yd. blue
½ yd. white
Additional fabric for border shown:
¾ yd. blue and ½ yd. white

To piece one block:

Piecing one block of Triangle Star is excellent practice for the methods used in all three-sided patchwork.

1. Cut three white or muslin triangles (3″).
2. Cut 6 dark diamonds (from 2¾″ strip).
3. Cut one 7½″ triangle from white or muslin.
4. Cut two 5¼″ triangles.
5. Sew two diamonds onto the small triangle as shown. Make three of these strips.

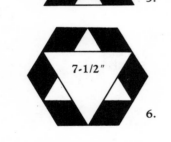

6. Sew these side strips on to the 7½″ triangle as shown.
7. To turn this hexagon block into a diamond, which is easy to assemble into a quilt top, sew the two 5¼″ triangles on opposite sides of the triangle star block.

To assemble TRIANGLE STAR quilt:

1. Piece 7 Triangle Star blocks.
2. Piece 4 corner blocks, using on one end two triangle halves cut from a 5¾″ triangle.
3. Piece 2 partial blocks for each end of the center vertical panel. The two triangle halves required are

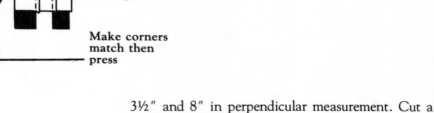

Wrong Side

Make corners
match then
press

3½″ and 8″ in perpendicular measurement. Cut a triangle this size and bisect it.
4. Sew the blocks into rows and assemble as shown.
5. Sew three 2″ strips of fabric into strata approximately 44″ long. Matching centers, sew the borders onto the quilt top from seam allowance to seam allowance. On the ironing board, let the bottom border lay out flat and straight. Fold the top border end under (right sides together) and pull it parallel to the bottom border. At the same time, carefully line up the strip corners for a good appearance. Then press with a hot iron to crease. Pin carefully in one or two places to hold in position. Open fold and sew along creased line, backstitching.

12 Star Quilt

See pg. 23 to assemble quilt
(3″ triangle size)
58″×84½″ without borders
70″×96½″ with borders

Borders:

3″ Silhouette Border;
(19 matching triangles on each short side; 29 matching triangles on each long side)

6″ border of medium blue.

Fabric requirements for 12-Star Quilt:

1 yd. light blue
1 yd. medium blue   approximate, may use scraps
1 yd. dark blue
6 yds. muslin

Fabric requirements for borders:

¾ yd. dark blue
1¾ yd. medium blue

Directions for blocks in 12 Star Quilt

1. Black-eyed Susan
pg. 18

2. Gear
pg. 18

3. Fireworks
pg. 19

4. Christmas Star
pg. 19

5. Flower Crown
pg. 20

6. Blooming Star
pg. 20

7. Wings of a Dove
pg. 21

8. Triangulation
pg. 21

9. Snowflake
pg. 22

10. Cabbage Rose
pg. 38

11. Compass
pg. 22

12. Unfolding Star
pg. 23

In all directions, light, medium and dark refer to fabric colors.

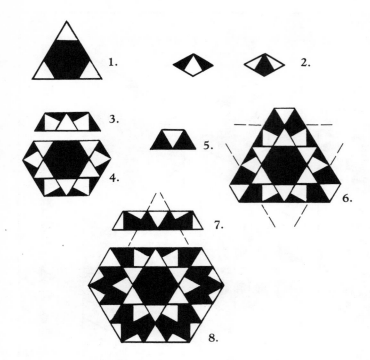

1. Black Eyed Susan

(3″ triangle size)

To piece one block:

1. Sew 3 light triangles onto one dark hexagon cut from a 5″ strip.
2. Piece 6 teardrop units and 6 teardrop units reversed.
3. Piece a strip from 2 teardrop units and a light triangle. Make 2 more like this.
4. Sew 1 strip on each side of the center triangle.
5. From 1 light and 2 dark triangles each, piece 6 flat pyramids.
6. Sew the pyramids onto three separate sides of the center hexagon.
7. Using the remaining teardrop units, and the remaining flat pyramids, piece 3 side strips.
8. Sew these on.

2. Gear

(3″ triangle size)

To piece one block:

1. Sew 3 medium triangles onto one light hexagon cut from a 5″ strip.
2. From dark and light fabrics, piece 6 teardrop units.
3. Piece a strip from 2 teardrop units and 1 medium triangle. Make 2 more like this.
4. Sew 1 strip on each side of the center triangle.
5. Cut 6 flat pyramids from a 2¾″ light strip at 5¼″ on the Clearview Triangle.
6. Cut 6 dark triangles and 6 light triangles. Piece in strips, 3 as shown in 6a and 3 as shown in 6b (using flat pyramids from #5).
7. Sew the smaller flat pyramids (6a) on 3 separate sides of the hexagon resulting from #4.
8. Sew the larger flat pyramids (6b) on 3 sides of the triangle resulting from #7.

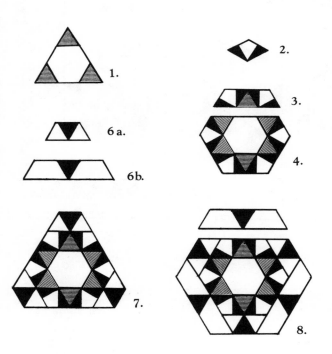

*As you do **any** piecing, press after sewing each seam if possible.*

3. Fireworks

(3″ triangle size)

To piece one block:

1. Sandwich piece 6 half-diamonds from dark and medium colors.
2. From 5¾″ strip, cut 6 dark triangle halves, 6 light triangle halves, and 6 medium triangle halves as shown.
3. Cut 6 diamond halves from a light 1⅞″ strip.
4. Sew the light and dark triangle halves together to make 5¼″ triangles.
5. Sew the diamond halves to the medium triangle halves as shown.
6. From one each of the units assembled in steps 1, 4 and 5, piece a triangle unit as shown. Make 5 more of these.
7. Sew the triangle units together in 2 sets of three.
8. Seam together across the middle, checking and pinning the center.

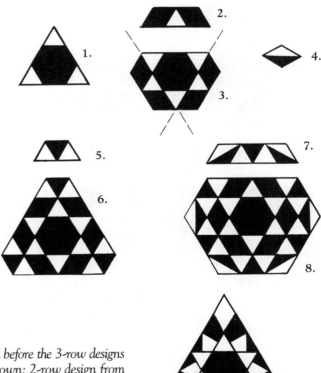

4. Christmas Star

(3″ triangle size)

To piece one block:

1. Sew 3 light triangles onto a dark hexagon cut from a 5″ strip.
2. From 3 light triangles and 6 dark diamonds, make 3 strips as shown.
3. Sew these strips on the three sides of the center triangle. (TRIANGLE STAR pg. 16).
4. From light and dark 1⅞″ strips, sandwich piece 6 half–diamond units.
5. From 2 light triangles and 1 dark triangle, make a flat pyramid as shown. Piece 5 more of these.
6. Sew 3 of the flat pyramids onto 3 separate sides of the TRIANGLE STAR.
7. Using 2 half–diamond units and 1 flat pyramid (from #5), piece a strip as shown. Make 2 more of these.
8. Sew 1 strip on each side of the triangle resulting from #6.

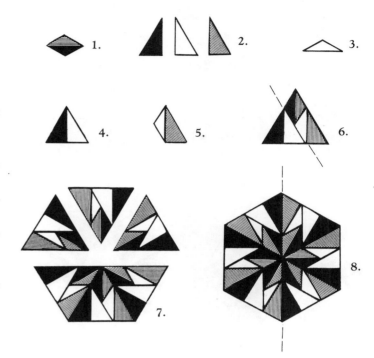

As all these blocks are assembled, 2-row designs are often created before the 3-row designs are complete. These 2-row designs could be other quilts. Example shown: 2-row design from BLACK EYED SUSAN assembled using 3 final strips that include light diamonds at the tips of the block. These triangular blocks would be arranged in rows with no setting strips.

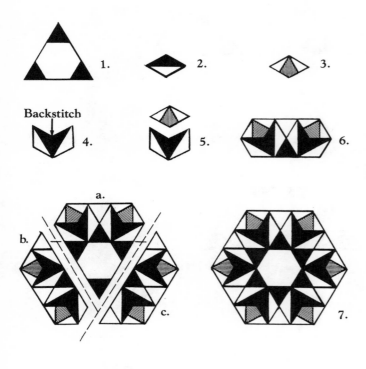

Backstitch

5. Flower Crown

(3″ triangle size)

To piece one block:

1. Sew 3 dark triangles onto 1 light hexagon cut from a 5″ strip.
2. From light and dark fabric strips $1\frac{7}{8}$″ wide, sandwich piece 12 half–diamond units.
3. From medium and light fabric strips $3\frac{1}{2}$″ wide, cut and piece 6 teardrop units (buds).
4. Sew 2 half–diamond units together as shown. Sew up to seam allowance only, stop, and backstitch. Make 5 more of these.
5. Set in teardrop units by hand or machine. Sew one side from edge to seam allowance, backstitch and cut thread. Pivot teardrop unit to other half–diamond unit, and sew from edge to seam allowance (flower).
6. From 2 flowers, a light triangle and a dark triangle, piece unit as shown. Make 2 more of these.
7. Seam these units to the center triangle as shown, adding 1 light triangle to the second unit and 2 light triangles to the corners of the third unit.

6. Blooming Star

(3″ triangle size)

To piece one block:

1. Sew 3 medium triangles onto 1 dark hexagon cut from a 5″ strip.
2. From 6 light diamonds and 3 medium triangles, piece 3 strips as shown.
3. Sew one strip on each side of the center triangle.
4. From light and dark fabric strips $3\frac{1}{2}$″ wide, sandwich piece 12 half–triangle units (6 right and 6 left).
5. From 1 dark triangle and 2 half–triangle units, piece a flat pyramid as shown. Make 5 more of these.
6. Sew this flat pyramid on 3 separate sides of the hexagon resulting from #3.
7. From 1 flat pyramid and 2 light diamonds, piece a strip as shown. Make 2 more of these.
8. Sew 1 strip on each side of the triangle resulting from #6.

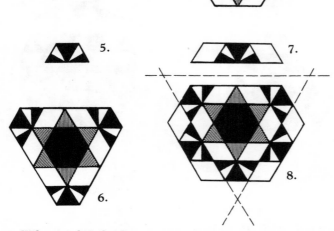

When making larger quantities of one block, more matching triangles, half-diamonds, etc., can be cut, pieced, and sandwich pieced in advance to save time.

7. Wings of a Dove

(3″ triangle size)

To piece one block:

(12 light diamonds and 24 dark triangles will be needed)

1. Sew 3 dark triangles onto a light hexagon cut from a 5″ strip.
2. From 1 medium diamond and 2 dark triangles, piece triangle as shown. Make 5 more like this.
3. Add medium diamonds and dark triangles as shown to make 3 sections.
4. Starting with the smallest, sew the sections onto the center triangle as shown.

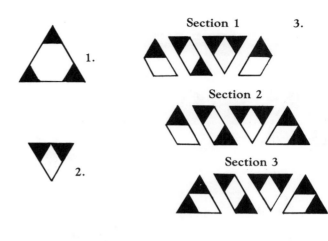

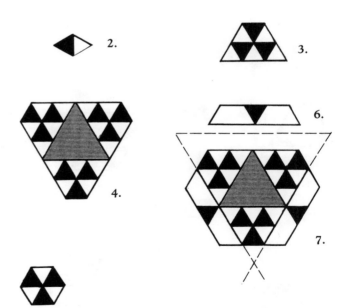

8. Triangulation

(3″ triangle size)

To piece one block:

1. Cut a 7½″ medium triangle.
2. From light and dark fabrics, sandwich piece 9 matching triangle units. Cut 6 light triangles.
3. Using 3 matching triangle units and 2 light triangles, seam this piece. Make 2 more of these.
4. Sew one unit on each side of the 7½″ triangle.
5. From light fabric strips 2¾″ wide, cut 6 flat pyramids at 5¼″ on the Clearview Triangle.
6. Using 2 flat pyramids and 1 dark triangle, piece a strip as shown. Make 2 more like this.
7. Sew 1 strip to each side of the triangle resulting from #4.

Each block in the 12-Star Quilt could be a separate quilt. However, it may be necessary to vary or eliminate the vertical and/or horizontal setting strips to bring out the best in each design. Another possible change would be to break up the center hexagon like this or some other way.

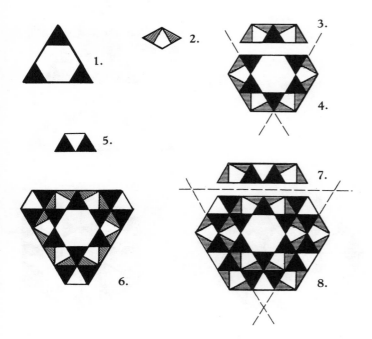

9. Snowflake

(3″ triangle size)

To piece one block:

1. Sew 3 dark triangles onto a light hexagon cut from a 5″ strip.
2. From 3½″ light and dark fabric strips, cut and piece 12 teardrop units.
3. Using 2 teardrop units and 1 dark triangle, piece a strip as shown. Make 2 more of these.
4. Sew 1 strip on each side of the center triangle.
5. Using 2 dark triangles and 1 light triangle, piece a flat pyramid as shown. Make 5 more of these.
6. Sew a flat pyramid to 3 separate sides of the hexagon resulting from #4.
7. Using 2 teardrop units and 1 flat pyramid, piece a strip as shown. Make 2 more of these.
8. Sew 1 strip on each side of the triangle resulting from #6.

10. Cabbage Rose

Directions on pg. 38

11. Compass (3″ triangle size)

To piece one block:

1. Sew 3 medium triangles to one light hexagon cut from a 5″ strip.
2. From 3½″ light and dark fabric strips, cut and piece 6 teardrop units.
3. Using 2 teardrop units and 1 medium triangle, piece a strip as shown. Make 2 more of these.
4. Sew 1 strip on each side of the center triangle.
5. Using 2 light triangles and 1 dark triangle, piece a flat pyramid as shown. Make 2 more of these.
6. Sew 1 flat pyramid to 3 separate sides of the hexagon resulting from #4.
7. From a 2¾″ light fabric strip, cut 6 flat pyramids at 5¼″ on the Clearview Triangle.
8. Using 2 flat pyramids and 1 dark triangle, piece a strip as shown. Make 2 more of these.
9. Sew a strip on each side of the triangle resulting from #6.

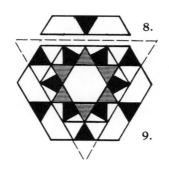

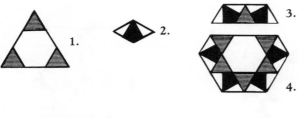

12. Unfolding Star

(3″ triangle size)

To piece one block:

1. Sew 3 light triangles to one dark hexagon cut from a 5″ strip.
2. From 1⅞″ light and dark fabric strips, sandwich piece 6 half–diamond units.
3. Using 2 half–diamond units and 1 light triangle, piece a strip as shown. Make 2 more of these.
4. Sew 1 strip on each side of the center triangle.
5. Using 2 dark triangles and 1 light triangle, piece a flat pyramid as shown. Make 5 more of these.
6. Sew 1 flat pyramid to 3 separate sides of the hexagon resulting from #4.
7. Sew a light diamond on each side of the remaining flat pyramids to piece 3 strips as shown.
8. Sew a strip on each side of the triangle resulting from #6.

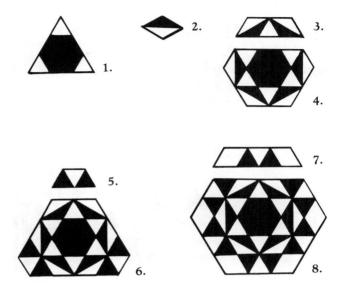

General Instructions

for assembling 12-Star Quilt, Peppermint Rose, and Cabbage Rose

To assemble a 12–block repeat quilt of any three–sided design that is based on three concentric rows of graph paper, including CABBAGE ROSE, PEPPERMINT ROSE, CHRISTMAS CACTUS, and any design in the 12–STAR QUILT (using 3″ triangle size; all measurements include seam allowance):

1. Sew 7½″ light triangle to opposite ends of the basic block (hexagon shape is changed into a diamond.)
2. Sew blocks together in vertical rows, 4 blocks to a row, with setting strips between blocks. (Setting strips are 2¾″ wide for PEPPERMINT ROSE and CABBAGE ROSE and 3″ wide for the 12-STAR QUILT. Other designs may need different strip widths.)

3. Add a fill–in piece to both ends of each vertical row. (A 30° triangle 16¾″ on the long size)

4. Sew the vertical rows together, inserting a strip between each pair of rows. Strip width for CABBAGE ROSE and PEPPERMINT ROSE is 5″. Vertical strip width for the 12–STAR QUILT is 3″ for the two inside strips and 3¾″ for the two outside strips.
5. Add the borders desired.

Snowflower

46″x49½″ (3″ triangle size)

CONSTRUCT FROM THE INSIDE OUT.

Fabric requirements:
1 yd. blue or dark fabric
2 yds. muslin or light fabric

To assemble SNOWFLOWER QUILT:

1. Sew 3 dark triangles to a light hexagon cut from a 5″ strip.

2. Piece 6 teardrop units as shown.

3. From 2 teardrop units and 1 dark triangle, piece a strip as shown. Make 2 more of these.

4. Sandwich piece from dark and light fabric 54 matching triangle units.

5. From 2 light triangles and 1 matching triangle unit assemble this triangle. Make 2 more of these.

6. Add strip from #3 as shown. Sew one of these units to each side of the center triangle.

7. Piece 12 teardrop units as shown.

8. From matching triangle units, light triangles, and teardrop units as in #7, assemble 3 large triangle units as shown. Sew one of these units to each side of the triangle resulting from #6.

9. Piece a star point from 6 matching triangle units and 4 light triangles as shown. Make 2 more of these.

10. Cut fill-in pieces for the star with sides measuring 12″ (see pg. 11). Assemble with star points as shown and seam onto the large triangle resulting from #8.

11. Trim rectangle to approx. 31½″x36″

12. Add a border of blue and white 1″ strips. Miter as on pg. 16. Add a 5″ border. Miter. Press.

5.

6.

8.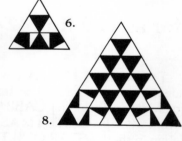

9.

Piecing Hints

All my piecing is done with ¼″ seams. Even if the presser foot on your sewing machine measures this ¼″ for you, it is a good idea to measure the seams occasionally until you are confident of accuracy. Check to be sure the seam is **just inside** the ¼″ line rather than right on it.

When many seams intersect at one point such as in the PEPPERMINT ROSE block, pinch the center where the seams cross, open the block to see how the seams are meeting and adjust as necessary. Pin to hold the block

for seaming.

A few tips about trimming seams are included in the cutting instructions. I trim in a number of places to reduce bulk as the quilt top is pieced. Be careful not to trim too much off before the next step, however, as the little points that stick out help align the parts for accurate sewing. Experience helps. The mild bias of the triangles also aids in lining up seams. Pull a little if necessary. All seams are pressed to one side to make quilting easier.

Trumpet Vine Wreath, 58½″×58½″. This quilt was designed and pieced by Mary Hickey, author of *Little By Little: Quilts In Miniature*. There is a lacy look to this elegant quilt design, echoed and emphasized by the printed border fabric. Anonymous quilter.

Christmas Tree, 32″×43″. This Christmas wall hanging could have pieces of jewelry pinned to it as additional ornaments. Or a child would enjoy getting a little wrapped gift from beneath this tree for every day of the month of Advent.

Precious Rose, 37″×40½″. This rose comes with many thorns, to make a star around the central block and a strong frame for the whole design. Lots of hand quilting adds to the rich texture of this wall hanging or crib quilt.

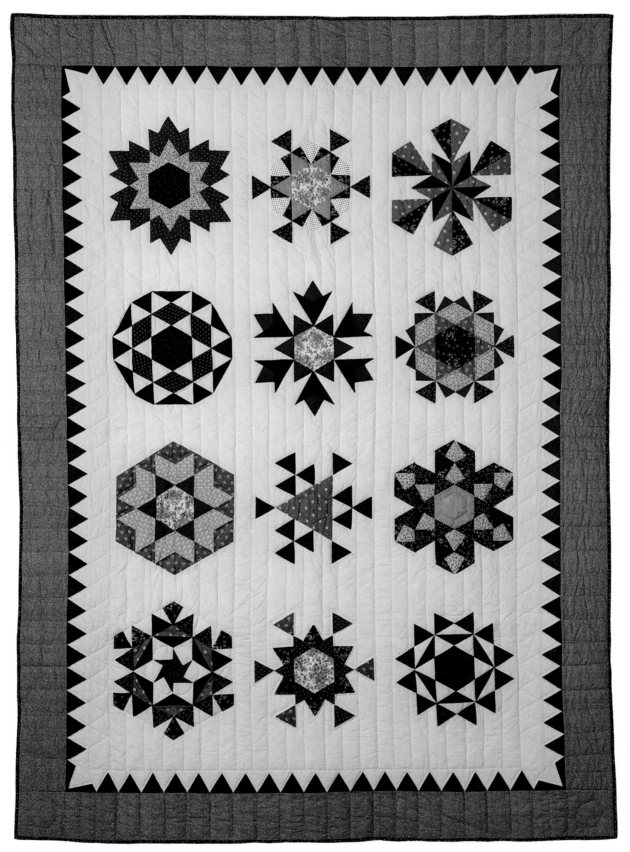

12-Star Quilt, 70″ ×96½″, begins to show the design possibilities of three-sided patchwork. Done in blue and white, the blocks look like snow crystals. Quilted by Maurine Eggertsen.

Snowflower, 46″×49½″, forms a flower in the center of the crystal. Other color choices could emphasize the hidden floral shape. A simple border was chosen, making this a quick quilt.

Triangle Star, 36″×42″, a bright little quilt, can be completely pieced, including borders, in less than four hours. Finishing by tying or machine quilting could produce a baby quilt or wall hanging in just one day. Quilted by Rose Herrera.

Silhouette, 54½″×63″, a bold star with feathered edges, is complemented by a strong frame. Use of a matching border stripe fabric adds a touch of elegance. This quilt takes approximately eight hours to piece.

Cabbage Rose, 79½″×100¼″, is closely quilted by the author with roses, rosebuds, leaves, branches and tendrils. The strong color scheme and graceful border add to the impact of this romantic quilt.

Peppermint Rose, 73″ ×93¾″, with its twirling rosebud blocks and leafy border, has a very floral appearance. Green and red are traditional, but a wide variety of colors and prints would be beautiful in this pattern. Quilted by Maurine Eggertsen.

Christmas Cactus, 67″ ×82½″. Strong in color, this quilt has a masculine, folk-art appearance. Some friends have been reminded of a West Coast Indian button blanket. The border is a strong frame for the lively blocks, and also quick and easy to piece.

Mayflower, 51″ ×55″, uses four appliqued stems to complete the graceful design. Red accents glow on this quilt that looks like a cut-paper valentine.

Bouquet, 57½″ ×69½″. Motifs from **Peppermint Rose** and **Cabbage Rose** combine in a medallion design. Pastel fabrics were chosen to emphasize a soft floral feeling.

Christmas Tree Star With Mistletoe, 72″×76¼″, is a sparkling quilt to wrap up in before a roaring winter fire, or to add to the bedcovers when it begins to get cold. A green and red color combination, or shades of red and black, would also be exciting in this design and appropriate to the season.

Tulip Garden, 46¼″×57″. Part of the center block is repeated in each corner for the look of a Hawaiian applique quilt. Contour or echo quilting would be a good choice to complete this quilt.

Precious Rose

37″ x 40½″ (3″ triangle size)

(1¾″ matching triangles make thorns around one block of CABBAGE ROSE)

CONSTRUCT FROM THE INSIDE OUT

Fabric requirements:
- ¼ yd. black
- ¼ yd. pink
- ¼ yd. green
- ¼ yd. assorted reds
- 1¼ yds. muslin

To assemble PRECIOUS ROSE QUILT:

1. Piece 1 block of CABBAGE ROSE as shown on pg. 38.
2. Cut six 5½″ triangles from muslin and add 1¾″ matching triangle units on 2 sides of each as shown.

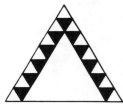

3. Sew these star points on 3 separate sides of the CABBAGE ROSE block.
4. Cut background pieces for the star 10½″ or longer on the side (see pg. 11).
5. Assemble 3 side sections from the star points and the background pieces as shown above. Sew to the center triangle. Trim edges to approximately 25¼″×30″.
6. Assemble a SILHOUETTE border from 2″ matching triangle units using corner pieces as given for CABBAGE ROSE (see pg. 39). Each short side needs 16 matching triangle units and each long side 18 units.
7. Add a 5″ muslin mitered border. Quilt with roses.

Note: Try not to stretch the rows of matching triangles while pressing them. If the matching triangles end up longer than the sides of the star points, ease them on.

Peppermint Rose

(3″ triangle size)
59½″ x 80¼″ without borders
73″ x 93¾″ with borders
See pg. 23 to
assemble quilt.

Fabric requirements:

½ yd. red
3 yds. green (may use 1½ yds. light green and
 1½ yds. dark)
6 yds. light background color

To assemble PEPPERMINT ROSE quilt: Make blocks and borders as instructed. Then see directions on pg. 23.

To piece one block:

1. Cut and piece for buds: 6 teardrop units in red and white.

2. Sandwich piece 18 half–diamond units in green and white. (Optional: piece 6 in dark green and 12 in light green.)

3. Cut 6 white 3″ triangles.
4. Sew 2 half–diamond units together along their light edges.
5. Sew 1 white triangle to the light edge of a half–diamond as shown.
6. Seam these 2 sections together as shown. Make 6 of these gem shapes in all.
7. Sew 3 gem shapes together, stopping at the outside seam allowance and backstitching. Sew the remaining 3 gem shapes together the same way.
8. Sew the 2 halves together from seam allowance to seam allowance, backstitching.
9. Carefully set in the teardrop units around the outside, by hand or machine.

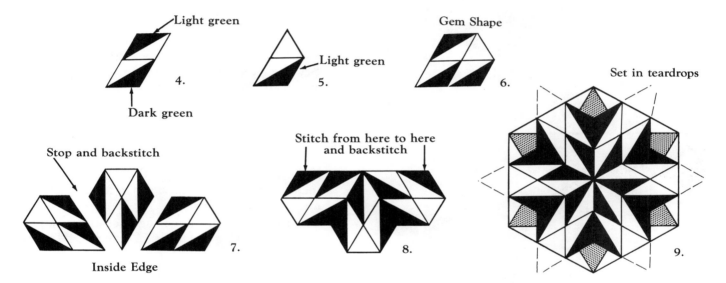

Setting in a teardrop unit:

1. Right sides together, sew the teardrop unit to one inside edge of a seamed pair of half-diamonds. SEW ONLY UP TO THE INSIDE SEAM ALLOWANCE AND BACKSTITCH.
2. PIVOT teardrop unit to match the two remaining raw edges. BACKSTITCH AND SEAM TO THE OUTSIDE EDGE.

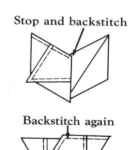

Stop and backstitch

Backstitch again

About Color

Many of the quilts in this book have been pieced in red and green, partly because this color scheme always suits a floral design. (Also it's a natural choice for a Christmas tree.) I have always like this combination. It's a classic color complement.

Another reason for choosing these colors is that they allow for strong contrasts making design and construction easy to see. Please feel free to try other hues in any of these patterns. Many beautiful effects are possible.

Always be aware of dark and light values when choosing colors for these designs. Think of what fabrics would look good in applique. Most small all-over prints will work easily into these designs. Large prints or regular geometrics can tend to break up the star or flower that is being pieced.

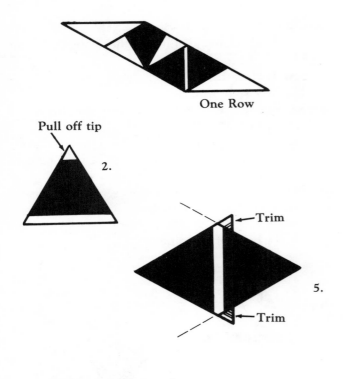

One Row

Pull off tip

2.

Trim

Trim

5.

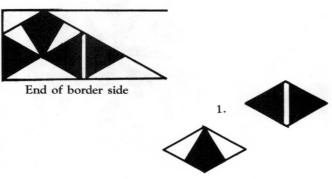

End of border side

1.

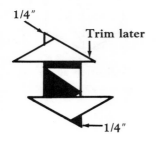

1/4"

Trim later

1/4"

To piece ROSELEAF border:

Each row consists of:
  2 diamond halves (cut from a $2^1/_8$" strip)
  1 teardrop unit
  2 green triangles with a white strip between (see below)
Piece 11 rows for each short side of the quilt.
Piece 15 rows for each long side.
Fill in the ends of the border sides as shown in diagram. The corners of the ROSELEAF border are squares the width of the border.

To piece the green triangles/white strip unit of the ROSELEAF border:

1. Piece a strata (set of strips):
   1" white or muslin
   $2^3/_4$" green
   1" white or muslin
2. Cut $3^1/_2$" triangles from this strata. Pull off the white tips.
3. Cut 3" triangles from a 3" green strip.
4. Sew the green triangle onto the white strip already seamed to the other triangle.
5. Press and trim off points shown.

To make the ROSELEAF BORDER go together more easily:

1. Make sure these 2 units are the same size. If not, increase or decrease seam width of teardrop unit to make it larger or smaller.
2. Sew the two above units together as you would diamonds, making sure the usual little triangle shows at the edge.
3. When putting the diagonal rows together pinch, check and pin to make sure the point of the teardrop is where the leaves touch each other.

Note: Because the 2-triangle piece is not a standard size, a larger than usual diamond half is needed at the top and bottom of each row in the border. Line up the angles as shown at the left, allowing the excess in the point to stick out. Trim this after the border rows are sewn together.

Add a final 3" border of background fabric cut on straight of grain. Measure quilt center width and length and mark the strips that length, pinning and easing as necessary.

Cabbage Rose

(3″ triangle size)
79½″ x 100¼″ pieced top with borders shown
59½″ x 80¼″ pieced top without borders
12 blocks are needed for this quilt.
Borders shown:
SILHOUETTE inner border 2″;
PEPPERMINT ROSE border using 3″ triangle;
2″ final strip cut on straight of grain.

See pg. 23 to assemble quilt.

Fabric requirements without borders:
¼ yd. pink or yellow
1 yd. red
1¼ yds. green
3¼ yds. muslin
⅓ yd. burgundy

Yardage requirements for borders as shown on CABBAGE ROSE quilt
½ yd. burgundy
½ yd. red
1 yd. green
3 yds. muslin

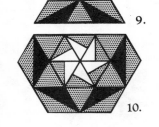
7.
8.

9.
10.

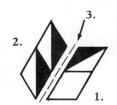
11.

12.

To piece one block:

1. Sandwich piece 6 half–triangle units in either red and pink or red and yellow. Sew together 6 right or 6 left.
2. Sandwich piece 6 half–diamond units in red and maroon, from $1^7/_8''$ strips.
3. Cut 6 red triangles.
4. Cut 12 green triangles. (When making a large quilt, speed–piece green and white pairs of matching triangles. You will need 72 sets for the large quilt.)
5. Cut 6 white triangles.
6. Cut and piece for rose leaves: 6 teardrop units in green and white.
7. Sew the 6 half–triangle units into a hexagon as shown.
8. Sew the 3 red triangles onto the hexagon to make a large triangle.
9. Make a strip as shown—from 1 red triangle and 2 red-and-maroon half–diamond units. Make 2 more strips like this.
10. Sew these strips onto the sides of the triangle.
11. Make a side piece from two green triangles and one white triangle. (Here you can use the matching triangles you have sewn.) Make 2 more of these. Sew these side pieces on separate sides of the hexagon as shown.
12. Make 3 more side pieces as in #11. Add two teardrop units to each, one on each side. Sew on as shown to complete the CABBAGE ROSE block.

Peppermint Rose Border for Cabbage Rose Quilt

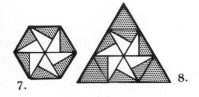

(3″ triangle size)

Each diagonal row consists of:
   2 white triangles
   1 white diamond
   3 green and white half–diamond units
   1 red and white teardrop unit
Diagonal rows may be assembled to the right or left.

To assemble one border unit:

1. Sew 1 white diamond to the light side of a half–diamond unit as shown.
2. Sew 2 half–diamond units together.
3. Seam 1 and 2 together only to seam allowance at the outside edge.
4. Set in rosebud (teardrop unit).
5. Add one white triangle at each end.

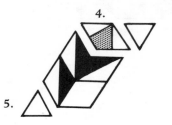

For the narrow SILHOUETTE border, (add to CABBAGE ROSE top before the PEPPERMINT ROSE border), speed–piece matching triangles from 2″ strips. You will need 40 matching triangle units for each short side and 54 for each long side. Proceed according to the directions on pg. 41.

To assemble PEPPERMINT ROSE border:

(I chose to use the same center piece on all four sides of my Peppermint Rose border. This resulted in approximately 2½" of excess border on the long side of the quilt, which did ease in. You may prefer to use center #1 from page 14 in the two long sides, to eliminate this problem.)

The short side of the border includes 2 corner assembly pieces, the center assembly, and a total of 10 rose units—5 right and 5 left. The long side includes 14 rose units—7 right and 7 left.

1. Sew corner assembly and reverse corner assembly on correct ends of border.

2. Measure for center point and quarter point both on border and side of quilt top. Mark with pins. Pin border to side at these marks. If there is fullness, mark the center of the remaining distances also, and pin there.

3. Sew border to side of quilt. Sew from seam allowance to seam allowance. Press to the outside.

4. Sew the corner assemblies together from seam allowance to outside (like a mitered corner). Adjust as necessary when seaming. Press. Fill corner with a piece cut to fit as on pg. 14.

5. Measure across the center of the quilt in each direction. Cut 2" strips and seam together end to end, a narrow border for each side of the quilt, plus about 6" for mitering. Mark end, center, and quarter points as before. Pin a strip to the pieced border, matching pins. Sew from seam allowance to seam allowance. Sew on with the pieced border underneath so the feed dog can help ease in fullness. Press thoroughly, using a press cloth or steam iron. Miter corner.

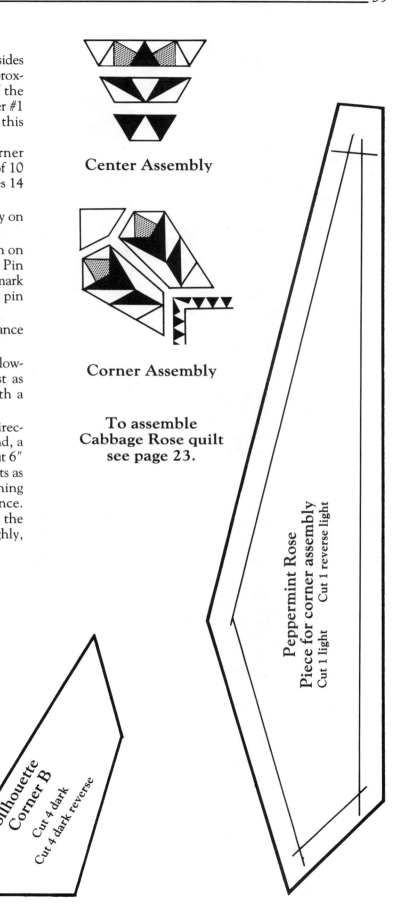

Center Assembly

Corner Assembly

**To assemble
Cabbage Rose quilt
see page 23.**

These templates include seam allowance

**Silhouette
Corner A**

2" triangle
Cut 4 light

**Silhouette
Corner B**
Cut 4 dark
Cut 4 dark reverse

**Peppermint Rose
Piece for corner assembly**
Cut 1 light   Cut 1 reverse light

Silhouette

54½"x63" (3" triangle size)

Fabric requirements:
  2 yds. light background color
  2 yds. dark fabric
  1⅔ yds. border strip

To assemble
SILHOUETTE QUILT:

1. Cut one 7½" dark triangle. Piece 12 teardrop units as shown. From 3" strips of light and dark fabric, piece 48 matching triangle units.

 1.

2. Construct a strip as shown, from 1 dark triangle, 2 light triangles, and 2 teardrop units. Make 2 more of these.

2.

3. Add matching triangles to strip #2 as shown and seam onto the 7½" dark triangle in order, starting with the shortest strip.

 3.

4. From a 5" strip of dark fabric cut 3 flat pyramids at 9½" on the Clearview Triangle. From 1 matching triangle unit and 2 light 3" triangles, piece the unit at right. Make 2 more of these.

 4.

5. 5.

5. Sew a 9½" pyramid to the pieced triangle #4. Press open. Make 2 more of these.

6. Trim the end of a 5" strip of dark fabric to a 60° angle. Sew this onto the triangle resulting from #5, press open, and trim the other end. Make 2 more of these.

 6.

7. Sew the 3 triangles resulting from #6 on each side of the center unit #3, as shown.

8. From dark fabric cut three 9½" triangles. Add strips of matching triangle units and teardrop units as shown to make 3 star points.

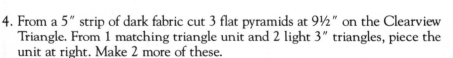 8.

9. From background fabric cut the fill-in pieces to turn the star into a rectangle. Cut them at least 18″ on the side (see pg. 11). Piece strips of matching triangle units. Extend as necessary with 2¾″ strips of background fabric. Sew pieced strips to the fill-in pieces as shown.

10. Assemble the star points and the fill-in pieces into the 3 sections shown. Seam onto the triangle resulting from #7 in order, with shortest section first.

11. Trim the star medallion resulting from #10 to approximately 42¾″x50½″.

12. Piece 66 matching triangle units. Make 2 rows of 18 each, and 2 rows of 15 each. Add 1 light triangle to the dark end of each row.

13. Sew the rows of matching triangles to the 4 sides of the medallion. Try sewing with the pieced strip under, to ease the triangles on. Press out.

14. Sew on the 4 corner pieces. Templates given on this page.

15. For the final border, sew a 5″ strip of dark fabric to all sides, mitering corners. (2 lengths of fabric for each long side, centering the seam and carefully matching stripe lines, etc.).

Silhouette Corner Diagram
Backstitch and pivot

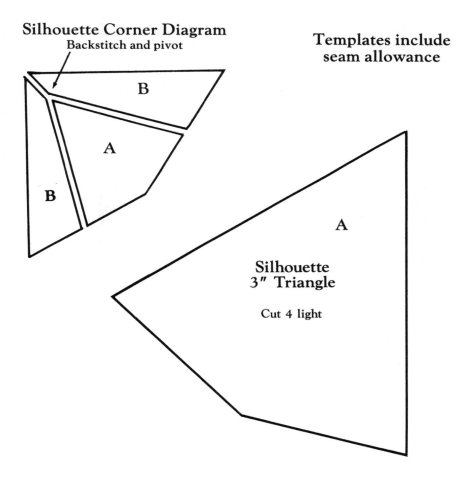

B

A

B

Templates include seam allowance

A

Silhouette 3″ Triangle

Cut 4 light

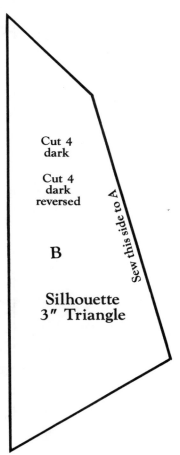

Cut 4 dark

Cut 4 dark reversed

B

Sew this side to A

Silhouette 3″ Triangle

Christmas Cactus

67"x82½"

(4" triangle size)

Fabric requirements:
½ yd. pink
1 yd. red
1½ yds. green
4¼ yds. black

To piece one block:

1. Cut 3 red and 3 green diamonds. (15 of each color will be needed for the whole quilt.) Sandwich piece 12 green and black half–diamond units. (60 will be needed for the whole quilt.) Piece 6 pink and black teardrop units. (30 will be needed for the whole quilt.)

2. From a diamond, a black 4" triangle, and 2 half–diamond units, piece a unit as shown. Make 5 more of these, alternating red and green diamonds.

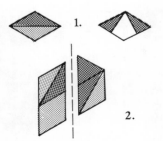

3. Sew three of the units made in #2 together, alternating the diamond colors. Sew only to the seam allowance and backstitch. Sew the other three together, backstitching. Stitch from seam allowance to seam allowance across the center, backstitching.

4. Set in blossom teardrops. Make 4 more blocks.

5. Cut ten 10½″ triangles* from black and sew onto opposite sides of each block.

*The CHRISTMAS CACTUS blocks I sewed had a tendency to encourage wider seams so the blocks ended up a little small. Then simply trim down #5 and #6 to match. All other instructions remain the same.

To assemble CHRISTMAS CACTUS:

6. Cut two 20″ wide* strips of black fabric. On each, trim one end to a 60° angle. Use on either side of the block in the center row. Then measure approx. 29″ from the center of the block to the outside edge, and trim to a straight edge. (Use the 60° trimmings, cut into 7″ strips, as part of the top and bottom outside border, #9 in instructions. See CHRISTMAS CACTUS diagram.)

7. Cut a 7″ strip of black fabric. Trim to a 60° angle and use as the setting strip between 2 blocks. Sew on and trim the end to the proper angle. Do the same for the remaining 2 blocks.

8. From black fabric cut one 14″ triangle, bisect, and use to finish the ends of one outside row of blocks. Use the angles cut from the center row to finish the ends of the other outside row.

9. Cut 7″ strips of black and add to the top and bottom of quilt, as shown in the diagram. Trim quilt top, without borders, to 53½″x69″. (But do not trim closer than 1″ to the blossom teardrops.)

Borders:

10. From 3¾″ strips of red and green fabric, cut flat pyramids at the 7¼″ line on the Clearview Triangle. Cut 28 of each color. Sew a black 4″ triangle to the end of each pyramid. Sew 14 left and 14 right of each color as shown.

11. Assemble into a row, inserting a diamond unit at center border as shown. (If the quilt top is wider than 54¼″, the top and bottom border will need adjustment to fit. One suggestion would be to insert a strip of fabric in the center diamond unit to widen the diamond. Another solution may be to insert a strip of the proper color fabric between the last flat pyramid in the row and the fill-in piece at the end of the row. Choose what looks best to you.) Cut 2 red and 2 green 7½″ triangles and bisect. Use these to straighten the row ends as shown in the diagram. Each short border contains 3 pairs of flat pyramids on each side of a green diamond center, and each long border contains 4 pairs of flat pyramids on each side of a red center.

12. To make the four corners, cut 2 squares of black fabric, 7⅜″ on a side. Bisect diagonally. (Or do this with paper and use as a pattern.) Also cut 2 squares each of red and green fabric 5⅜″ on a side. Bisect diagonally, sew as shown, placing the colors to match the fill-in pieces. Add to the ends of the short rows and sew these on the quilt last.

*Measure the width of the block and vary from 20″ as necessary.

Backstitch

3.

4.

5.

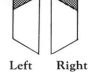

Left   Right

10.

Center
Diamond
Unit

11.

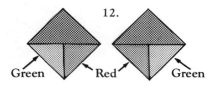

Green   Red   Green

12.

Left and Right Corners

Trumpet Vine Wreath

58½"x58½" (3" triangle size)

by Mary Hickey

Fabric requirements:

- ¾ yd. light green
- ¼ yd. dark green
- ¼ yd. light peach
- ¼ yd. dark peach
- 2½ yds. muslin
- 1½ yds. border stripe

To assemble TRUMPET VINE WREATH quilt:

The TRUMPET VINE WREATH is made up of 6 wedge-shaped units. To make one wedge:

1. From muslin cut three 3" triangles and one 5¼" triangle. From a 2¾" strip of muslin cut a long diamond at 5" on the Clearview Triangle. Cut one side, mark on the other side, and trim to a 60° angle (see pg. 7).

2. Sandwich piece 3 half-diamond units in light green and muslin. (50 needed for whole quilt.) Sandwich piece 1 half-diamond unit in dark green and muslin. (14 needed for the whole quilt.) Sandwich piece 2 half-diamond units in dark peach and muslin. (12 needed for the whole quilt.)

3. Cut and piece 1 teardrop unit in light peach and muslin as shown.

3.

4. Sew 2 dark peach half-diamond units together along their dark edges. Sew only to seam allowance and backstitch.

5. Set in the teardrop unit.

6. Sew on a 3" muslin triangle as shown.

7. Stitch a light green half-diamond unit to a dark green half-diamond unit as shown.

8. Sew #7 to #6 as shown.

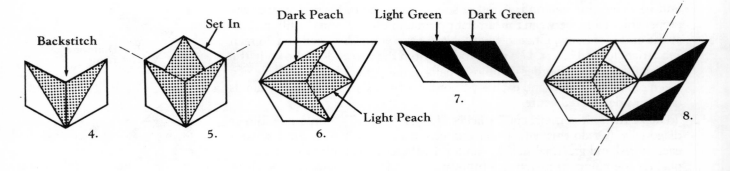

Backstitch

Set In

Dark Peach

Light Green   Dark Green

Light Peach

4.   5.   6.   7.   8.

9. Stitch the large muslin triangle to the blossom-leaf section (#5).

10. Sew a light green half-diamond unit to the long diamond as shown. Add this to #9.

11. Sew two 3″ muslin triangles to a light green half-diamond unit. Add to #10 to complete the wedge. Make 5 more of these wedges.

12. Sew the wedges together in 2 sets of three. Sew these together across the center.

13. Cut two 12½″ muslin triangles. Bisect these. Stitch these triangle halves to the wreath as shown (see quilt diagram).

14. From muslin, cut 2 strips 5¼″ wide and sew to the 2 long sides. Cut 2 strips 3½″ wide and sew to the 2 other sides.

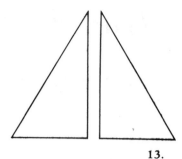

13.

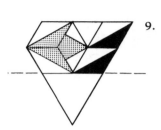
9.

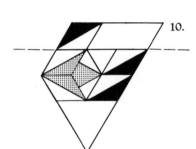
10.

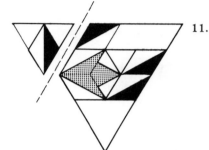
11.

Borders:

15. From 2¾″ strip of muslin, cut 8 flat pyramids at 7½″ on the Clearview Triangle. Cut and piece 16 teardrop units from light peach and muslin as shown. (Sandwich piece various half-diamond units as listed in #2 if you have not already done this.)

16. Sew a dark green half-diamond unit, a flat pyramid, a teardrop unit, and light green half-diamond unit in a strip as shown.

17. Sew a teardrop unit, a light green half-diamond, a 3″ muslin triangle, and 2 light green half-diamond units in a strip as shown.

18. Sew the 2 strips (#16 and #17) together as shown to create one bud section. Make 7 more of these units.

19. From muslin, cut four 5¼″ triangles. Sew a triangle between 2 bud sections. Cut 8 triangle halves from 5¾″ muslin triangles. Use as fill-in pieces at the border ends. Make 3 more borders.

20. Sew 2 borders to opposite sides of the quilt top. Cut 4 squares of muslin, 5″ on the side. Sew a square to each end of the remaining 2 bud borders. Sew these borders to the quilt top. Add 2 more borders: (1). A 2½″ strip of muslin; and (2). a 7½″ wide strip of printed fabric. (Can be mitered as in TRIANGLE STAR, pg. 16.)

15.

Dark Green   **16.**

17.

18.

19.

Mayflower

51"x55" (3" triangle size)

Fabric requirements:
   ⅛ yd. accent color
   ¼ yd. red
   1¼ yds. maroon print
   3¼ yds. background color
   (3¾ yds. if mitering corners of
   final border)

To assemble MAYFLOWER quilt:

1. Assemble the center hexagon from red and pink 3" triangles. Add background triangles on 3 separate sides.

2. Cut 10 red diamonds and add 2 background triangles to each as shown.

3. Sandwich piece 20 half–diamond units from maroon and the background color. Add a background diamond and a half–diamond unit to both sides of #2 as shown. Make 2 more of these.

4. Sandwich piece approximately 82 matching triangle units from pink and maroon. To 1 matching triangle unit, add one background triangle. Make 2 more of these. Add to the bottom of #3.

5. Add strips as shown to each side of #4.

6. Add 3 of #2 (as shown in the MAYFLOWER diagram) to 2 of 5. Then sew these 3 sections to the center triangle (#1) in order, with the smallest first.

7. Cut six 5¼" triangles from background fabric. Add strips of matching triangle units and 3" maroon triangles as shown to make 6 star points.

8. Sew 3 star points to 3 separate sides of the hexagon resulting from #6.

9. Cut two 120° triangles from a 7" strip of background fabric. (These are 2 of the fill-in pieces.)

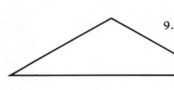

Assemble the 4 corner fill-in pieces:

10. From 5" strips of background fabric, cut 4 large diamonds. Add a strip made from a maroon diamond and a background diamond as shown. Make 2 of these. Make 2 reverse.

11. Cut stem from maroon fabric and applique as shown (stem template, pg. 47). Applique the inside curve first, then the outside. Applique all the way to the fabric edge at the top of the stem. At the bottom, applique only to within ½" of the bottom edge of the diamonds, leaving 3¾" free on the stem.

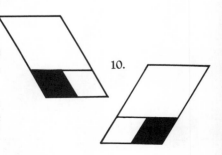

11.

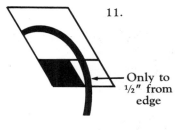

← Only to ½″ from edge

12. Assemble flower unit from 2 half–diamond units, one #2, two 3″ background triangles, 1 background diamond, and a triangle half from an 8″ triangle. Make 2 reverse.

13. Sew #11 to #12 as shown, catching end of stem in seam. Add 3½″ strip of background fabric across the bottom, turning stem ends back out of the way.

14. Combine 3 star points and the 6 fill-in pieces to make the 3 side units shown in diagram. Seam these onto the center triangle #8.

15. Pin back stem ends and trim quilt top into a rectangle measuring approximately 31¼″x37″. Applique remaining stem ends, trimming as necessary. Add SILHOUETTE BORDER with reversed corner. You will need 11 matching triangle units for each short side and 13 matching triangle units for each long side. Add a final border of 7½″ strips of background fabric. Miter corners if desired.

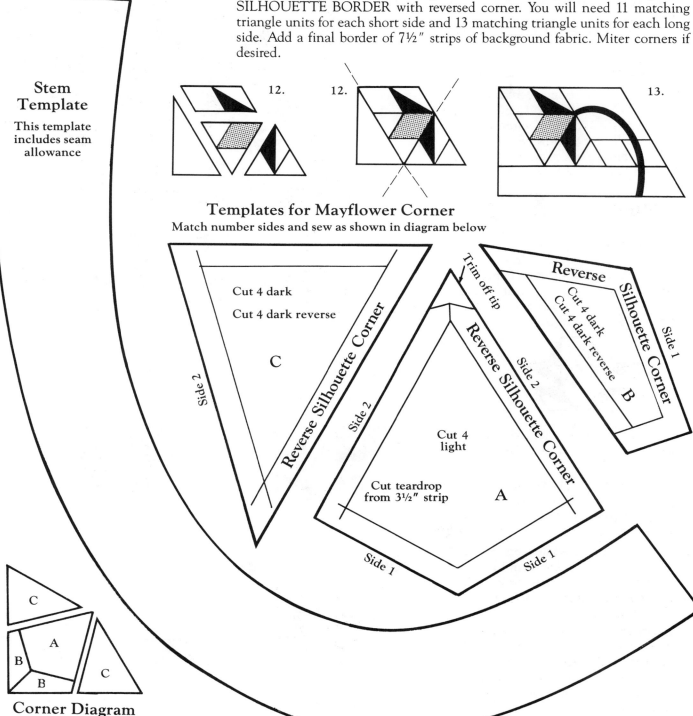

Stem Template

This template includes seam allowance

Templates for Mayflower Corner
Match number sides and sew as shown in diagram below

Corner Diagram

Bouquet

57½″x69½″ (3″ triangle size)

Fabric requirements:
$^{1}/_{8}$ yd. light pink
$^{1}/_{8}$ yd. dark pink or maroon
$^{2}/_{3}$ yd. red
1 yd. green
4 yds. light background color or white

To assemble BOUQUET QUILT:

1. Sandwich piece from green and white fabric 92 half-diamond units. Also piece 34 red and white teardrop units. Assemble unit as shown from 1 white 3″ triangle, 1 white diamond, and 2 half-diamond units. Make 6 of these.

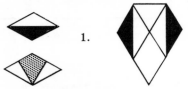

2. Add a row of 2 half-diamond units on the right and left as shown, stitching only up to the seam allowance at the top, and backstitching.

3. Set in 2 teardrop units and add two 3″ white triangles on the corners as shown.

4. Sew on a 5¼″ white triangle at the bottom. Make 5 more of these.

5. Piece 24 green and white teardrop units.

6. Add a 2¾″ strip of white fabric to the top of #4. Trim corners and add a green 3″ triangle to each corner. (Or cut a flat pyramid at 12″ on the Clearview Triangle.)

7. Construct a strip as shown using 2 white triangles, 2 green triangles, 2 green and white teardrop units, and 1 flat pyramid cut from a 2¾″ strip at 7½″ on the Clearview Triangle. Make 5 more of these.

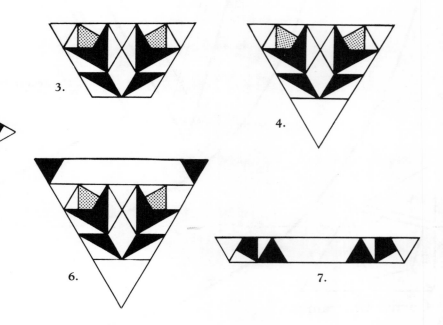

8. Add this strip to the top of #6.

9. From a 5″ strip of white fabric, cut 6 gem shapes. Add a green triangle opposite the point of each.

10. Sew together 2 rows of half-diamond units as shown. Stop and backstitch at top seam allowance. Set in red and white teardrop unit. Add two white 3″ triangles, top and bottom. Make 5 more of these straight flowers.

11. Assemble 6 other gem-shaped units from 1 red and maroon half-diamond unit, 2 green triangles, a green and white teardrop unit and a white triangle at the left of the teardrop.

12. Piece together into 6 columns as shown in the BOUQUET diagram: a straight flower (#10), a gem shape (#9), and other gem shape (#11). Add a green triangle and a green and white teardrop unit at the top, and the indicated sections of the red CABBAGE ROSE at the bottom.

13. Assemble the columns and the triangle-shaped pieces resulting from #8 into 6 wedges as shown in the BOUQUET quilt diagram.

14. Sew into 2 half-hexagons, left and right of the dotted line. Seam together across the middle.

To assemble the corners:

15. Use the remaining flower teardrops and green and white half-diamond units. From background fabric cut:
    Four 9¾″ triangles
    Eight 5¼″ triangles
    Eighteen 3″ triangles
    Thirty triangle halves from 3½″ strips
    Two triangle halves from two 8″ triangles.
    Assemble 2 each right and left corners as shown. Sew these corners onto the center hexagon.

16. Add a final border of 8½″ strips of white (or light background) fabric. A scalloped border may be a good choice for this pretty quilt.

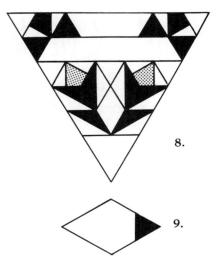

8.

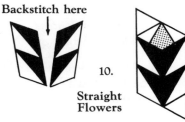

9.

Backstitch here

10.

Straight Flowers

11.

Gem Shape

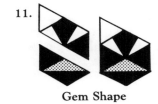

12.

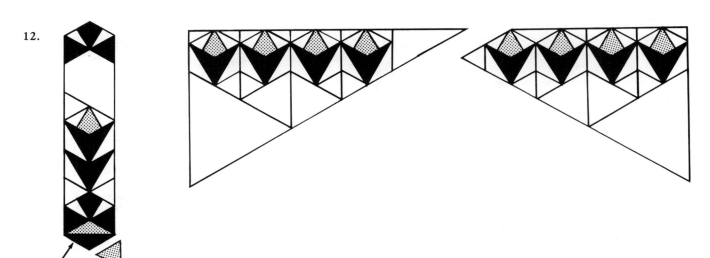

Left

Red Triangle For Cabbage Rose Center (Alternate left or right)

Tulip Garden

46¼"x57" (4" triangle size)

Fabric requirements:
   ¾ yd. flower color
   1⅓ yds. leaf color
   2¼ yds. background color

To assemble TULIP GARDEN quilt:

1. From $2\frac{3}{8}$" strips of the leaf fabric and the background fabric, sandwich piece 12 half-diamond units. (32 will be needed for the whole quilt.)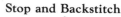

2. From $2\frac{3}{8}$" strips of the flower fabric and the background fabric, sandwich piece 12 half-diamond units. (28 will be needed for the whole quilt.)

3. From $2\frac{3}{8}$" strips of the leaf fabric and the background fabric, cut diamond halves, 6 of each. Cut more as needed for the rest of the quilt.

4. From the flower fabric and the background fabric, piece 6 teardrop units as shown. (14 will be needed for the whole quilt.)

5. Cut 12 triangle halves from 7¾" triangles of background fabric.

6. Assemble a strip and its reverse—flower half-diamond unit, leaf half-diamond unit, diamond half—as shown at right. Seam together up the center, stop at the seam allowance and backstitch. Sew the large background triangle halves on the right and left sides of the pair of pieced strips. To complete the shape, set in a flower teardrop at the end. Piece 5 more of these.

7. Sew the pieces assembled in #6 together in sets of three. Then seam together across the middle, matching centers carefully. To 2 opposite sides of the TULIP GARDEN block, sew two 13¾" triangles cut from background fabric.

8. Construct corners as shown. Each corner is pieced from: 4 flower half-diamond units, 6 leaf half-diamond units, one 7¼" background triangle, 2 flower teardrop units, 1 leaf diamond half from a 2⅜" strip, two 4" background triangles, and 1 triangle half cut from a 6½" triangle of leaf fabric.

9. Cut four 3¾" strips of background fabric, selvage to selvage. Cut four diamond halves from a 6" strip of background fabric, extending the Clearview Half-Diamond with a ruler.

10. Assemble the quilt top as shown. Add the 6" diamond halves to the completed corner pieces. When sewing these on, overlap the diamond halves, seam, and trim.

11. Add 3" strips of the leaf fabric for a border.

Stop and Backstitch

6.

Dark   **Light**

Set In

6.

Set In →

Set In

8.

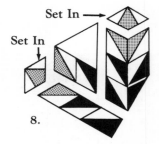

4" Triangle Added

Corner   8.

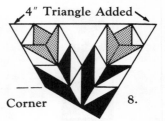

8.   **Reverse Corner**

Christmas Tree Star with Mistletoe

76¼″ × 72″ (3″ triangle size)

Fabric requirements:

1¼ yds. blue-purple
1¼ yds. blue left & right borders
2 yds. bluegreen tree color
1¼ yds. muslin
1⅓ yds. black

To assemble CHRISTMAS TREE STAR WITH MISTLETOE quilt:

1. From muslin cut one 7½″ triangle and three 3″ triangles. Cut 6 black diamonds. Assemble 1 block of TRIANGLE STAR (see pg. 16).

2. From bluegreen cut six 5¼″ triangles and six 9¾″ triangles. Cut a 2¾″ strip of black and of bluegreen. Trim both strip ends to a 60° angle. Seam the 2 strips together lengthwise, with the trimmed ends lined up. Rotary cut 2¾″ slices from the pair of strips at a 60° angle. Seam these together into diamond units as shown. Make 6 of these.

3. Sew bluegreen 5¼″ triangles to 3 separate sides of the TRIANGLE STAR block.

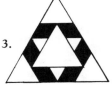

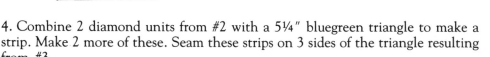

4. Combine 2 diamond units from #2 with a 5¼″ bluegreen triangle to make a strip. Make 2 more of these. Seam these strips on 3 sides of the triangle resulting from #3.

5. Sew three 9¾″ bluegreen triangles to 3 separate sides of the hexagon resulting from #4. This completes the center triangle. All other piecing now will be to assemble the 3 outside sections, which includes the borders and fill-in pieces.

Fill-in pieces:

6. From blue-purple fabric cut two 120° triangles that are 12″ perpendicular (piece one of these). These are the other 2 fill-in pieces.

7. From a 2¾″ strip of black cut 36 diamonds and 12 flat pyramids (cut at the 5¼″ line on Clearview Triangle). Cut eight 7½″ blue-purple triangles and 4 blue-purple triangle halves (from bisected 10¼″ triangles).

Piece One

8.

8. Use 6 muslin 3″ triangles, one 7½″ blue-purple triangle, 3 black diamonds and a black flat pyramid to assemble a Mistletoe block as shown. Make 7 more of these. Also assemble 4 partial blocks, omitting the large triangle and adding a 3″ triangle of muslin. Seam together in 4 groups of three, putting the partial block always on the right side. Add the 10¼″ triangle half at left or right row end as shown. Add a 5″ strip of blue-purple across the top of each mistletoe unit, trimming to 60° angle. On the angled end of the mistletoe unit, seam on a 2¾″ strip of blue-purple. Trim to correct angles.

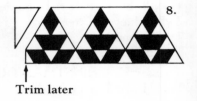

8.

Trim later

To add star edges and star points to fill-in pieces:

9. From black, cut twelve 3″ triangles. Also cut from black thirty 5¾″ triangles, and bisect them. From 1⅞″ strips of muslin, cut 60 diamond halves. From muslin cut forty-eight 3″ triangles. Sew a black 5¾″ triangle half, a muslin triangle, and a muslin diamond half into a strip as shown. Make 3 more of these. Sew into a row. Make 5 more rows. Make reverse strips to make 6 reverse rows.

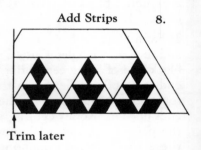

Add Strips   8.

Trim later

10. From bluegreen and black, sandwich piece 36 half-diamond units. Assemble into a row of three, with a white triangle at 1 end and a black triangle at the other end. Make 5 more of these. Also sew 6 reverse rows.

11. Put row #9 and row #10 together to make 6 star edge units and 6 reverse star edge units.

12. Sandwich piece from 1⅞″ strips of muslin and black 12 half-diamond units. Cut 2 muslin triangles, 10 muslin diamonds, 6 black 3″ triangles, and 6 muslin flat pyramids (from 2¾″ strip at 5¼″ on the Clearview Triangle). Assemble star point as shown. Make 3 more of these. Make 2 star points with triangles at the tip instead of diamonds. Adding star points and star edge units to fill-in pieces to make 3 outside sections:

Strip   Reverse Strip

9.

13. Sew star points to a star edge and a star reverse edge as shown. Sew these strips to a left Mistletoe piece. Sew only to the seam allowance at the center and backstitch. Make another one of these. Sew center edge seams.

14. Use only one star point on the right Mistletoe piece. Leave 3-4″ unseamed when attaching the star edge (darker line). Make another one of these.

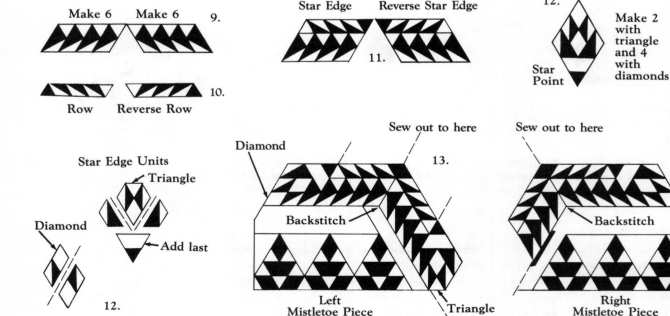

15. Attach 2 star edges to each side fill-in piece, leaving 3″ unseamed on each side (darker line).

16. Sew a 9¾″ bluegreen triangle to #15 as shown. Make a left and a right. Add the correct Mistletoe piece to each one. Then finish the partly-sewed seam.

17. Seam right outside piece to center (#5). Seam left outside piece to center triangle. Press. Finish the partly-sewed seams.

18. Sew top outside piece to body of quilt. Press. Finish the partly-sewed seams. Trim the left and right sides even. Quilt should measure approx. 58½″×60¾″. Add a 10″ border of bluegreen (tree color) to the top and bottom. Add an 8″ border of medium blue to left and right.

Christmas Tree

32″x43″ (2″ triangle size)

Fabric requirements:

¼ yd. red (may use scraps)
¼ yd. dark green
½ yd. medium green print
1/8 yd. spotty green print
2¼ yds. light-colored background print

To assemble Christmas Tree Quilt:

1. Assemble 1 block of CHRISTMAS STAR for the top of the tree (see pg. 19), substituting 2″ triangle size and following the rules given. Use red fabric.

2. Add two 4½″ triangles of background fabric to opposite sides of the star.

3. Sandwich piece approximately 102 matching triangle units, mixing combinations of the three green fabrics and the background fabric.

4. From 3″ red strips, cut 7 hexagons.

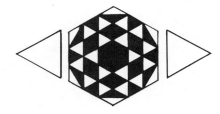

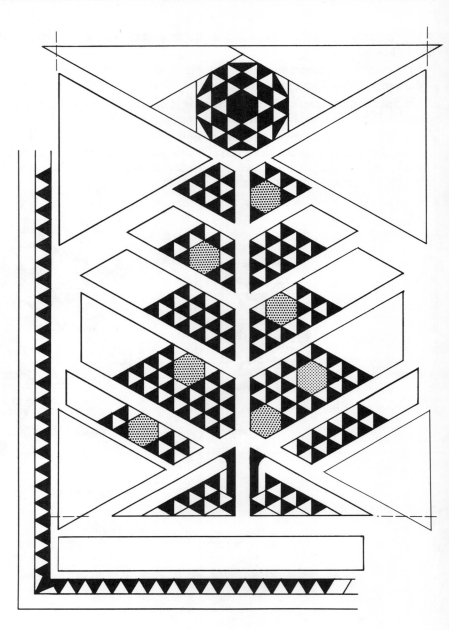

5. Assemble the hexagons, matching triangle units, and dark or light 2″ triangles as necessary into 10 tree branches as shown on the diagram above.

6. Cut from background fabric and add to the right and left branches as shown in the diagram:
   2nd row from top — 2 long diamonds cut from 3″ strip with the longer side measuring 5⅛″.
   3rd row from top — 2 long diamonds cut from 4¼″ strip with the longer side measuring 6¼″.
   4th row from top — 2 flat pyramids cut from 5½″ strip at the 8¼″ line of the Clearview Triangle.
   Bottom row   — 2 flat pyramids cut from 3″ strip at 5¾″ line of the Clearview Triangle.

7. Sew the branches together in order on the left and on the right side. Add a 9½″ triangle of background fabric to the bottom of both sides as shown.

To assemble base of tree:

8. Piece the left and right sides of the base as shown, using a 1¾″ strip of background fabric, matching triangle units, 2 dark triangles and 2 diamond halves from background fabric for each side.

9. Cut and sew together lengthwise: a $1\frac{1}{8}''$ strip of background fabric and a $1\frac{1}{8}''$ strip of dark green. Trim one end at a 60° angle, with the green longest. Sew on a 2″ background triangle.

10. Sew #9 to the left or right tree base (#8). Trim at the top as shown.

11. Sew a dark green triangle at the top and a diamond half and green triangle at the bottom center as shown.

12. Sew the left and right tree base to the left and right branch sections.

13. Sew the tree together up the center. Stop and backstitch at the top center seam allowance.

14. Sew two 12″ triangles of background fabric to the left and right top of the branches.

15. From a 7″ strip of background fabric, cut two 120° triangles. Sew onto the CHRISTMAS STAR as shown in the diagram.

16. Set in the star at the top of the tree, sewing to the seam allowance at the center and backstitching. Then pivot the star to the other side of the tree and sew from the seam allowance to the edge. Trim off the little tips of the 120° triangles as shown. Trim off the bottom triangles as shown, even with the tree base, and add a 3¾″ strip of background across the bottom. Trim the top to 2″ from the star.

17. Add a 2″ SILHOUETTE border and a final plain border of 1¼″ strip of background fabric cut on straight of grain.

14.

7.

Left Side

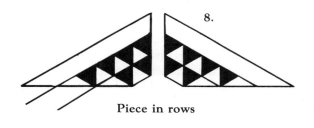

8.

Piece in rows

2″ Triangles   9.

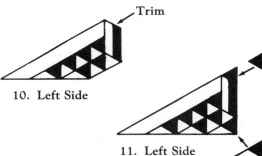

Trim

10. Left Side

11. Left Side

Index

About the Author

Sara Nephew began her artistry in metalwork. After receiving a B.A. degree in Fine Art, she worked for a commercial shop, repairing and designing jewelry, and invented a new enamel-on-brass technique. Her cloisonné work has appeared in national exhibits. She has since turned her interests to quilting, in large part, because of her fascination with the myriad textures and colors of fabrics. In 1984 she started her own business repairing, making, and selling quilts and wall hangings. Since the publication of her first book, *Quilts From a Different Angle,* her quilts have received national attention. Sara's second book, *My Mother's Quilts: Designs from the Thirties,* kindled renewed interest in depression-era quilts.

Sara lives in Snohomish, Washington, with her husband, Dale, and their three children. She is active in two local quilt guilds, Quilters Anonymous and Busy Bee Quilters.